RHODE SCHOOL of CUISINE

RSC

 **$50** *Certificate*  **$50**

We do hope you will enjoy **FROM OUR TABLE TO YOURS**.

This voucher offers you a $50 discount on the published rate of any of our current cooking school courses. You can combine vouchers to an upper limit of $300 per person, per week. Please see reverse for details.

The course is always such great fun and we would be delighted to see you there soon.

Mike & Terri

TERMS AND CONDITIONS

Validity
This certificate is valid for a discount of $50 for the bearer against any single week course
offered by the Rhode School of Cuisine in any location.

Surrender
Certificates must be used for final payment.
They must arrive with the final payment eight weeks prior to arrival at the school to be valid.
Certificates cannot be used for the initial deposit.

Aggregation
Certificates may be aggregated or used with any other discount, to a maximum of $300 value off the
normal published price for any single week for any individual.

Transfer of Certificate
Certificates are valid until surrendered and may be transfered i.e. the Certificate is valid for the bearer.

Subject to Availability
The Rhode School of Cuisine will honor certificates even when notification of the use of
the certificate is made after the booking. However use of the Certificate is strictly subject to
availability of the week and location desired.

Booking Procedure
The client must book direct with the Rhode School of Cuisine main office in order to use the certificates.
Certificates may only be used on bookings originated directly with the Rhode School of Cuisine
main office or via the internet – see contact list below.

Contact Details
Rhode School of Cuisine Main Office: Tel: +44 1428 68 51 40
Toll free from the US: 1 888 254 1070   Fax: +44 1428 68 34 24
email: info@rhodeschoolofcuisine.com
www.rhodeschoolofcuisine.com

RHODE SCHOOL of CUISINE

RSC

Hope you had a great time at
Villa Lucia and Rhode School of Cuisine

The Staff

First published in Great Britain in 2001 by the
International Culinary Society Network Limited

Text © Michael Rhode 2001
Photographs © Rhode School of Cuisine 2001
Design and layout © Rhode School of Cuisine 2001

A CIP catalogue record for this book is available
from the British Library

ISBN 0-9541008-0-8 Hardback
ISBN 0-9541008-1-6 Softback

Text set in ITC Galliard

Designed by Jim Gowland
Creative Heads, Covent Garden

Photography by Thierry Cardineau 2001
Food preparation by Frédéric Rivière
Watercolours by Christelle Riethmuller
Typesetting by Trevor Gray

Printed in the United Kingdom
at the Cambridge University Press

FROM
OUR
TABLE
TO
YOURS

Recipes from the
French Mediterranean
and Tuscan Hills

Frédéric Rivière
(Le Mas des Oliviers, France)

An exciting and innovative chef, Fred is the head chef of the Rhode School of Cuisine and has been running courses in the South of France since 1996. After obtaining his professional diploma from the prestigious *Les Sorbets*, his creative skills were developed at impressive French restaurants *Père Bise* and *La Pyramide* as well as *La Bourride*, *Auberge du Jarrier* and *Heilly Lucullus* in Avignon. Fred's artistic ability and attention to detail personify his attitude towards cooking and food presentation. Fred practises classic French techniques with a contemporary influence to give his dishes color, flavor and decorative style. His belief in simple ingredients and ability to use different regional specialties in each recipe, makes Fred's classes appealing to those who want to learn traditional methods as well as some new and creative ideas.

Giancarlo Talerico
(Head Chef, Tuscany, Italy)

Originally from Milan, Giancarlo graduated from the *Instituti Alberghiero di Stato* and spent the following few years working in exclusive restaurants in this exciting Italian city. After leaving Milan he joined a cruise line company for many years as a top chef and gained extensive insight and knowledge into international cuisine. Returning to Italy, Giancarlo's rich Italian background and desire to master areas of Italian cuisine were nurtured at the *Maestro Di Casa* in Milan. His use of traditional methods that have been handed down from generation to generation epitomizes the essence of great Italian and true Tuscan cuisine. Giancarlo believes that cooking is not about following recipes but about your senses and love of food. His love of great food and passion for imparting his culinary knowledge on to others makes him a valuable member of the Rhode School of Cuisine team.

Alvaro Maccioni
(Guest Chef)

Alvaro is the owner of London's *La Famiglia*, a restaurant he started back in 1975 and which has now became a popular eating place for the rich and famous and those seeking authentic Italian cuisine. Alvaro has a passionate belief in only using fresh produce and traditional methods of cooking. Alvaro believes that *"if a chef cooks like his mother, he is a great chef. If he cooks like his grandmother, he is even greater"*. The fact that Alvaro's restaurant is still fashionable after more than twenty years says something about *La Famiglia*'s food and the man himself. A true food historian, Alvaro will tell his students about the only two distinctive styles of cooking in Italy – Tuscan and Venetian. In 1998 Alvaro published *Mamma Toscana*, an authentic Tuscan cookbook.

We believe the best way to experience the culture of a country is through its cuisine. In learning about food and cooking, you travel down varying paths of discovery, from delicate ones that tickle your palate to steep, rocky ones that bring you to new savory lands.

For many of you, it's with our cookbook that you start your journey with our imaginative and traditional French and Italian recipes. Others have traveled the distance overseas to stay with us for a week at our villas where the Rhode School of Cuisine chefs have captured their senses while exploring French and Italian culture and cooking.

Wherever it is you start your journey with us, we hope to continue to offer new and exciting paths for you to wander down, whether it is an exciting twist to a classical recipe or a visit to our new luxurious Palazzo in Marrakech. The core of our philosophy is to open the door to traditional cultures through their cuisine. We hope you find that this book will provide an insight into our philosophy and tempt you to voyage further.

We wish you successful ventures into our recipes, from our table to yours.

Best wishes,

Mike & Terri Rhode

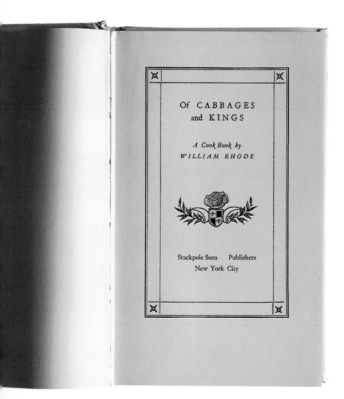

Of CABBAGES
and KINGS

A Cook Book by
WILLIAM RHODE

Stackpole Sons   Publishers
New York City

The love of food has always been strong in my family. My father, Bill, and his sister, Irma, both wrote cookbooks. Living in Manhattan in the 1930s they founded a catering business with their friend James Beard, who went on to become a gastronome of world renown. I like to imagine my father serving canapés at some grand social function, thereby meeting my mother and falling in love. It probably didn't happen like that, but it would be in keeping with the importance of food in the lives of my family.

In 1938, my father wrote a cookbook called *Of Cabbages and Kings*, a collection of anecdotes and recipes from the tables of European royalty. In 1941, he wrote a second book, *This Business of Carving*. Soon after, he became one of the first editors of *Gourmet* magazine. Unfortunately, he died at an early age, while I was still young, so other than an enthusiasm for food, he was unable to pass much of his culinary knowledge on to me.

Aunt Irma, however, was able to impart a few "bachelor recipes" directly to me when I was starting out in life, just as she had taught my father the basics of the kitchen when he was young. A formidable woman and cook, Aunt Irma wrote many cookbooks, several for the *Time/Life* series. In the 1950s, she again teamed with James Beard to found a cooking school, and I have included one of her fabulous recipes and one from my gastronomous grandmother.

Thinking of Aunt Irma and James Beard reminds me of a wonderful evening we shared late in their lives. My brother and I were in New York for her 80th birthday, and Mr. Beard invited us all to dinner at Danny Kaye's famous restaurant. Not only did Mr. Kaye enthusiastically cook and serve our dinner himself, which was a great thrill in its own right, but also it was also nice to see Mr. Beard and Aunt Irma sitting at the end of the table, together again.

It seems to me an odd coincidence that my father would entitle a book *Of Cabbages and Kings*. The title comes from the poem "The Walrus and the Carpenter" by Lewis Carroll, whose writing I have always loved. "The time has come," the Walrus said, "to speak of many things, of shoes and ships and sealing wax, and cabbages and kings, and why the sea is boiling hot and whether pigs have wings." I especially like the end of the poem when they eat all the oysters – but then I'm fond of oysters. Here is one of my favorite tales from my father's book.

When Emperor Constantine, the last of the truly absolute rulers, held court in Byzanz, his judicial methods were at times strange, and frequently highhanded, with complete disregard for the status, rank, or nationality of an alleged culprit.

Because of superstition, it was a breach of court etiquette to turn over a fish during a meal. Fish were served whole in those days, so a guest was expected to finish one fillet, remove the middle bones, and then attack the other side. Superstition held that ill fortune would befall the imperial household if ever, in the presence of the Emperor, a fish should be turned on a plate.

One day, a representative of France was among the guests of the Emperor. The fish course was served, and at the crucial moment the French emissary, unaware of that strange bit of etiquette, calmly flipped his fish over to tackle the other side. The Emperor's major-domo issued a horrified moan, and the Emperor actually jumped from his chair, trying to break the jinx by rising from the table where this ghastly offense had occurred. Guards quickly appeared, and the bewildered Frenchman was thrown in the dungeon.

A few days later the Emperor decreed his death. In those days, since there were few means of communication, international courtesy did not exist; the Frenchman was definitely on his own, with his neck out, so to speak. But strange justice has its own strange rules. One such rule was the famous "last wish before death".

The Emperor and the entire court were assembled to watch the offender's execution, hoping his death might appease the gods. Any last wish was allowed to the poor Frenchman, except to spare his life. The condemned man smiled and made his request to the Emperor: that everyone who had seen him turn the fish should have his eyes burned out with a hot iron poker.

Consternation befell the assembly, and the denials of having seen anything during the ill-fated meal came fast, until even the Emperor admitted that his sudden rise from the table was probably due to indigestion. The Frenchman was released, and he returned to France in great haste.

The French ambassador escaped the wrath of Constantine, but of course the oysters did not escape from the Walrus and the Carpenter. The poem and the story remind me that food is important, but dining should be first and foremost a pleasure. They also connect me to my family history. All of this is what we do every day at the Rhode School of Cuisine, and it is what we hope to do with this cookbook. As the previous generation of my family did, we wish to pass our love, enthusiasm, and knowledge of food on to you, *from our table to yours.*

AUNT IRMA'S CHICKEN
IN WINE

Preparation time: 10 minutes
Cooking time: 40 minutes
Serves 4–6 people

6 BONED CHICKEN BREASTS
2 OZ/55 G BUTTER
1 LARGE ONION
2 BAY LEAVES
1 CUP OF DOUBLE (HEAVY) CREAM
1 CUP CARROTS (*JULIENNE*)
1 LB/450 G MUSHROOMS
½ CUP PORT
½ CUP SHERRY
2 TBSP EACH OF BUTTER AND FLOUR (*ROUX*)
SALT AND PEPPER TO SEASON
3 SPRIGS OF PARSLEY

Arrange the chicken breasts in a shallow baking pan.
Cover liberally with butter, and sprinkle with salt and
pepper. Add the sliced onions and bay leaves. Bake at
390°F/200°C for approximately 40 minutes, the
chicken should be golden brown when done. Remove
the chicken from the pan and place in a casserole dish.
To make the sauce, place the pan that was used to
cook the chicken on a very low heat, add 1 cup of
heavy cream, the port, sherry, sliced mushrooms,
carrots, and stir. Thicken the sauce with the *roux*. Pour
the sauce over the chicken and warm in the oven until
ready to serve.

Serve sprinkled with parsley.

GRANNY'S
FUDGE PIE

Preparation time: 15 minutes
Cooking time: 30 minutes
Serves 4–6 people

4 OZ/115 G BUTTER
8 OZ/230 G SUGAR
2 EGGS
2 OZ/55 G DARK BAKING CHOCOLATE (95% COCOA)
½ CUP CREAM
½ TSP OF SALT

Melt the chocolate in a *bain-marie*. Separate the eggs,
place the 2 egg yolks in a bowl, slowly add the sugar
and butter and combine, add the melted chocolate and
cream. In a separate bowl beat the 2 egg whites until
stiff with ½ teaspoon of salt. Blend the egg whites
into the chocolate, sugar and butter mixture. Grease
6 individual ramekins or small pie tins, pour in the
mixture and bake at 330°F/170°C for approximately
30 minutes.

Serve with vanilla ice cream.

At the Rhode School of Cuisine, we offer cooking holidays for people who love food, and this cookbook is intended to be an extension of that experience. Like our classes, this book shares delicious recipes, useful techniques, and helpful tips from our expert chefs. As with the cultural excursions that are scheduled during the week at the Rhode School of Cuisine, we hope the brief introductions for each recipe will give you some of the cultural and historical background needed to broaden your education. And like our guests, we hope you will be inspired and have fun along the way. Although, this book cannot provide you with luxury accommodation at one of our spectacular villas, we do hope it will be the catalyst you need to come and join us.

We believe cooking, like art, is a creative process. Enjoying a fine meal is akin to walking through a gallery, soaking up the ambiance, lingering to marvel at certain pieces, and savoring the experience. Cooking is similar to art, not only in its consumption, but also in its production. As the painter chooses colors, the cook chooses flavors. Consider the names for a painter's range of colors and a gourmet's sense of taste; is it purely coincidence that the former is called a palette and the latter is a palate?

At the Rhode School of Cuisine encouraging creativity is our ultimate goal. We hope that exposing you to a variety of flavors and combinations will inspire you to be creative in your own cooking. Perhaps you will find ingredients or techniques that you can adapt to some of your favorite recipes, making them more authentically French or Italian. As you look through *From Our Table to Yours*, we encourage you to experiment, to look for new ideas, and to create your own masterpieces.

Holidays with the Rhode School of Cuisine are designed to be fun, informative, relaxing, and luxurious. Ideally located in beautiful villas, our schools offer a special combination of beauty, tranquility, and cultural attractions. Cooking classes are conducted by our expert chefs, who involve each guest in the preparation of every meal. Whether they are novices or skilled cooks, guests leave with the culinary knowledge and skills needed to make the chef's delicious recipes.

At the Rhode School of Cuisine, we use cuisine as a way to introduce our guests to the rich cultures of the country they are visiting. Weekly schedules feature frequent cultural excursions such as guided tours of Florence in Italy and wineries in France. Each school's location offers a wealth of cultural amenities.

Excerpts from the journal of a guest of the Rhode School of Cuisine:

"The view! Every morning, I rush to the window, eager to throw open the shutters and take in the incredible view as the sun highlights the Mediterranean spread out before me. We enjoy breakfast out on the terrace, and it seems each of us is

trying to suppress a silly grin, struggling to soak in the beauty that surrounds us, and waiting for the morning's lesson.

Fred is such a creative chef. Most of the recipes we learn are his own creations. I shouldn't have been intimidated about learning French cuisine. Though some of his recipes are very intricate, Fred patiently takes us through each one, and with his instruction, we all learn what's required for the preparation – and the beautiful presentation – of each dish.

We eat lunch on the terrace, proud of the meal we prepared, as the sun reaches its peak above us. This afternoon, we're off to visit the Picasso Museum in Antibes as well as the ancient city of St Paul de Vence. Yesterday we visited a local winery. Our charming guide led us on a fascinating tour of the grounds and the production facilities. Tomorrow, Fred is taking us to the open-air market, and we'll help him select the fresh ingredients for our dinner.

And the food! We're here for the food, right? We're eating so well and learning so much. Each afternoon, we go into the kitchen and learn to prepare a delicious three-course meal. After dinner, we go out to the terrace to enjoy the cool breeze and the local liqueurs, or adjourn to the living room and enjoy the view."

Brian Falk

We are often asked, "Which location would you choose to go to?" when a client is struggling with the choice. We find this question exceedingly difficult to answer because the setting and experience at each school is so different. Would you prefer to savor your fresh ravioli on the poolside terrace nestled against the Tuscan hills and olive groves? Or perhaps you prefer the soft touch of the Mediterranean breeze as you gaze out to sea while sipping on a glass of *vin blanc*? Whichever experience you choose, it is our role to welcome you with open arms and provide five-star service with a smile.

French Cooking

Contents

Italian Cooking

French Cooking

Mastering the Art of French Cooking was a famous cookery manual of the mid-twentieth century. Its premise, perfectly respectable in its time, was that *la cuisine française* was complete and that it had rules which could be taught.

In recent decades, our understanding has grown more sophisticated. We realize that France boasts not one, but several styles of cooking. *Haute cuisine, cuisine bourgeoise, cuisine régionale*, and *cuisine moderne* may be flags of convenience, but they identify distinctive styles and influences.

Each category, of course, can overlap another. A professional chef in a luxury restaurant will probably prepare, say, *petits farcis niçois* (stuffed baby vegetables), differently from the home cook. Both may be equally talented in their own ways, but their approaches might be diametrically opposed. One may stick to a family recipe going back four generations. The other could be pushing back the boundaries of his or her imagination and technical skill.

Restaurant cooking began in the twentieth century under the influence of a famous chef, Auguste Escoffier, who codified professional practice in his *Guide Culinaire*. What he taught, the emphasis on stocks, sauces, garnishes and techniques is still relevant today. His codification of dishes and methods, though, has been superseded by generations of chefs who, having absorbed his lessons, are prepared to take them a stage further.

Instead of copying classic dishes, they reinterpret them. If they are creative, they don't hesitate to experiment. Chefs like Michel Bras or Marc Veyrat use a palette of wild plants that would never have been used in the Grand Hotels of yore. In the hands of a Pierre Gagnaire, exotic flavorings, which never appeared in the old *Répertoire de Cuisine*, are adopted into a French context and enrich it.

Despite the rapid changes that have occurred in restaurants, home cooking has remained closer to its roots. Ask most Frenchmen what they would like for a Sunday lunch and the answer will probably be "*Gigot d'agneau rôti*", or a leg of lamb spiked with garlic, roasted rare and accompanied with *flageolet* beans tossed in the meat's juices. And at least once a week, they expect a *bifteck frites* (steak and fries).

Family cooking, whether in the towns or in the countryside, still clings to simple classic dishes, the salade verte with a perfect vinaigrette, the *boeuf bourguignonne*, the *tarte aux pommes*. They are the nation's comfort food, and France is unique in having so many wonderful recipes on which it can call for its routine, day-to-day eating.

Historians may attribute the French pre-eminence in gastronomy to royal courts where monarchs expected their *maîtres queux* or master chefs to devise luxurious, culinary flights of fancy. The truth is that the fresh produce; whether fruit, vegetables, meat, poultry, game or seafood, is the key.

Purple raspberries sold on the Quai St Antoine in Lyons in summer, mesclun under the roof of Forville in Cannes, wriggling *crevettes grises* from La Rochelle, sparkling rockfish from Marseille or Toulon, *poulet de Bresse*, veal from Limousin – the list of exceptional raw materials runs to hundreds. Then there are the *fromages* and the *charcuterie*. If you enjoy food, it's impossible not to be excited by what you can find in the smallest market in the smallest village.

Michael Raphael

Les soupes

SOUPS

"Of all items on the menu, soup is the one which exacts the most delicate perfection and strictest attention."
Auguste Escoffier

Nowhere in the world has a richer repertoire of soups than France. From nourishing, self-contained meals to delicate broths served as tasters in chic restaurants, they span every season, every region, every eating occasion. There are thickened soups: *purées, veloutés, crèmes* and seafood *bisques*. There are limpid *bouillons* and consommés. There are hearty, chunky soups inspired by the *jardin potager* (the vegetable garden), and there are the celebrated seafood soups: bouillabaisse, *bourride* or *cotriade* all inspired by the sea.

Choosing the right kind of soup to serve and knowing how to present it is as important as knowing when to wear casual clothes and when to be formal. A demitasse of *citrouille en velouté* (page 19) with a cappuccino topping might be perfect for a refined dinner party. The same soup served in the pumpkin shell, perhaps with *croûtons*, could be a fun starter when entertaining friends. Served simply in a bowl, it's an ideal autumn supper dish.

La citrouille en velouté

CREAM OF PUMPKIN SOUP

La citrouille/pumpkin grows all over France but is especially popular in Lyons and Provence. Paul Bocuse, France's most influential chef of the twentieth century, popularized this classic winter soup by serving it inside the pumpkin skin.

Soup ingredients
1 LB 5 OZ/595 G PUMPKIN
3½ OZ/100 G ONION
2¼ OZ/60 G CELERY
2½ PT/1½ LITERS CHICKEN STOCK
4 TBSP/2 FL OZ/60 ML OLIVE OIL
4 TBSP/2 FL OZ/60 ML DRY WHITE WINE
1 GARLIC CLOVE
1 *BOUQUET GARNI*

Garnish
6½ TBSP/3½ FL OZ/105 ML *CRÈME FRAÎCHE*
(HEAVY OR SOUR CREAM)
FRESH CHIVES
FRESH CHERVIL LEAVES

Seasoning
SALT
WHITE PEPPER

Preparation time: 50 minutes
Cooking time: 25 minutes
Serves 4 people

Peel the pumpkin. Cut three quarters of it into large cubes, and the remainder into a *brunoise* and set aside. Peel and dice the onion, celery and garlic.

Heat the olive oil in a large frying pan (skillet); add the diced onion, celery and garlic. *Sauté* over a medium heat for approximately 2 minutes, without allowing the vegetables to color. Add the large cubes of pumpkin and continue to cook for 5 minutes. Season with salt and white pepper and *déglacer* with white wine. Simmer to reduce slightly.

Next add the chicken stock and *bouquet garni* and leave to simmer for 30 minutes. Leave to cool and place all of the ingredients into a blender and blend until smooth. Pass through a fine sieve.

When ready to serve, reheat the soup and add the *brunoise* of pumpkin, continue to heat until the pumpkin becomes soft. Stir in the *crème fraîche* and check the seasoning. The soup can be served in a small pumpkin or squash that has been hollowed out. Garnish with freshly chopped chives and serve with grilled *croûtons* brushed with olive oil.

Consommé de crustacés et sa julienne de légumes sous croûte

SHELLFISH CONSOMMÉ WITH A JULIENNE OF VEGETABLES UNDER A PUFF PASTRY SHELL

Traditionally shellfish soup was prepared from a *purée* made from the meat and shells of crustaceans. Frédéric Rivière has retained the concentrated flavor of the respected classic recipe, but lightened it by using a broth whose aromas are sealed in until the pastry crust is broken.

***Bisque* ingredients**
1 LB 2 OZ/500 G VARIETY OF SMALL SHELLFISH AND LEFT OVER SHELLS (LOBSTER, LANGOUSTINES, CRAB, GREEN CRAB AND SCAMPI TAILS)
4 TBSP/2 FL OZ/60 ML OLIVE OIL
4 TBSP/2 FL OZ/60 ML COGNAC
6½ TBSP/3½ FL OZ/105 ML DRY WHITE WINE
2¼ OZ/60 G CARROT
2¼ OZ/60 G LEEK
2¼ OZ/60 G ONION
2¼ OZ/60 G FENNEL
9 OZ/255 G TOMATOES
1 TBSP/½ FL OZ/15 ML TOMATO CONCENTRATE
2 GARLIC CLOVES
1 *BOUQUET GARNI*
2 STEMS FRESH TARRAGON

***Julienne* ingredients**
2¼ OZ/60 G CARROT
2¼ OZ/60 G LEEK
2¼ OZ/60 G ZUCCHINI
OLIVE OIL AS REQUIRED
BOUQUET GARNI

Crust ingredients
7 OZ/200 G PUFF PASTRY
2¼ OZ/60 G FLOUR
1 EGG YOLK

Seasoning
1 TSP/5 G SAFFRON
SALT
BLACK PEPPER

Preparation time: 1 hour 30 minutes
Cooking time: 1 hour
Serves 4 people

For the *bisque*, peel all the vegetables and cut into *mirepoix*. Heat the shellfish (meat left in the shells) in a frying pan of very hot olive oil for a couple of minutes and then add *Cognac* and *flambé*. *Déglacer* with white wine and reduce until almost no liquid remains. Add the *mirepoix* of vegetables, tomato concentrate and continue to cook for 5 minutes. Place the contents of the pan into a large pot and add enough water to cover all ingredients. Next, add the crushed garlic, *bouquet garni*, tarragon, salt and black pepper, bring to a boil. Skim off any impurities that may rise to the surface. Leave to simmer for 1 hour. Pour the mixture through a fine sieve lined with cheesecloth and then bring back to a boil, skimming the surface as necessary. Stir in the saffron and set aside.

For the *julienne*, peel and cut all the vegetables into a julienne. Cook each vegetable separately in three different pots, using olive oil, *bouquet garni*, salt, and pepper until *al dente*.

Place a mixture of the *julienne* vegetables and the *bisque* into the individual ovenproof bowls. Cover with a round of puff pastry slightly larger than the bowl. Seal the pastry around the bowl with beaten egg yolk, and brush the top with the remaining egg yolk. Bake in a preheated oven at 390°F/200°C for approximately 20 minutes or until the crust is golden brown.

Crème de céleri à l'huile de truffe et aux fèves

CELERY VELOUTÉ WITH TRUFFLE OIL AND BEANS

"During my years as a cooking instructor, I have noticed that celery seems to be a forgotten ingredient. I created this easy to prepare soup, which will surely be remembered for its delicacy of flavor".

Frédéric Rivière

Celery *velouté*
13½ OZ/385 G CELERY ROOT, PEELED AND CUBED
1¾ OZ/50 G SHALLOTS
2 GARLIC CLOVES
1¾ FL OZ/50 ML OLIVE OIL
6½ TBSP/3½ FL OZ/105 ML DRY WHITE WINE
4 CUPS/1¼ LITERS VEGETABLE *BOUILLON*
13 TBSP/6½ FL OZ/195 ML *CRÈME FRAÎCHE*
1 *BOUQUET GARNI*
1 EGG YOLK

Garnish
7 OZ/200 G FAVA BEANS
1½ TBSP/½ FL OZ/15 ML *TRUFFLE* OIL
¾ OZ/20 G CHOPPED CHIVES

Seasoning
FINE SALT
BLACK PEPPERCORNS

Preparation time: 35 minutes
Cooking time: 1 hour
Serves 4 people

Sauté the shallots and garlic in olive oil and butter. Add the celery root, salt and pepper. *Déglacer* with the white wine and reduce. Add the vegetable *bouillon* and *bouquet garni*. Cook for 35 minutes, and then add the *crème fraîche* and cook for an additional 10 minutes. Remove the *bouquet garni*, blend the mixture and adjust the seasonings to taste. Stir in the egg yolk just before serving.

For the garnish, shell the beans and cook in boiling water for 2 minutes. Cool in ice water, and remove the skins and reserve.

Place the beans in the bottom of a bowl. Cover with the *velouté* (with egg yolks added) and sprinkle with the chives and a few drops of *truffle* oil.

La soupe de poissons du marché de Forville

PROVENÇAL FISH SOUP

This soup had its origins in Marseille, where small rockfish caught in the rocky inlets, *calanques*, were a cheap source of food. Now they have become almost a luxury. Every chef along the coast adds his own *touche personnel* to the basic recipe. Frédéric Rivière's is a tribute to Cannes' covered fresh produce market, Forville, one of the finest on the French Riviera.

Soup ingredients
1 LB 5 OZ/595 G SMALL ROCKFISH
3½ OZ/100 G CONGER EEL (OR SIMILAR EEL)
2¼ OZ/60 G CARROT
2¼ OZ/60 G LEEK
2¼ OZ/60 G ONION
2¼ OZ/60 G FENNEL
1¼ OZ/35 G CELERY
5¼ OZ/150 G TOMATOES
6½ TBSP/3½ FL OZ/105 ML OLIVE OIL
3 GARLIC CLOVES
1½ OZ/45 G TOMATO CONCENTRATE
1 SPRIG OF TARRAGON
1 *BOUQUET GARNI*
ZESTE FROM ½ AN ORANGE
1 SPRIG OF BASIL
2 SPRIGS OF FLAT PARSLEY
6½ TBSP/3½ FL OZ/105 ML DRY WHITE WINE
3½ TBSP/1¾ FL OZ/50 ML *COGNAC*
3 STARS *ANISE*
3¼ TBSP/1½ FL OZ/45 ML *PASTIS*

Aïoli
1 EGG YOLK
1 TSP MUSTARD
6½ TBSP/3½ FL OZ/105 ML OLIVE OIL
3½ TBSP/1¾ FL OZ/50 ML SUNFLOWER OIL
1 TBSP VINEGAR
6 GARLIC CLOVES, CRUSHED
SALT AND PEPPER TO SEASON

Rouille
2¼ OZ/60 G POTATO
1 EGG YOLK
1 GARLIC CLOVE
1 TSP HOT PEPPER PASTE/HOT CHILLI PASTE
6½ TBSP/3½ FL OZ/105 ML OLIVE OIL
4 TBSP/2 FL OZ/60 ML SUNFLOWER OIL

Garnish
12 ROUNDS OF FRENCH BREAD
3 TBSP/1½ FL OZ/45 ML OLIVE OIL
5 OZ/140 G PARMESAN
2¼ OZ/60 G CHOPPED FLAT PARSLEY

Seasoning
SALT
10 SECHUAN PEPPERCORNS
½ TSP/2 G SAFFRON

Preparation time: 1 hour 30 minutes
Cooking time: 35 minutes
Serves 4 people

For the soup, clean the fish and eel and cut into pieces. Peel and cut the vegetables into a *mirepoix*. Heat the olive oil in a frying pan and *sauté* the fish for 3 minutes. Add the *mirepoix* of vegetables, crushed garlic cloves and tomato concentrate, and sweat the mixture for another 2 minutes. Pour in the *Cognac* and *flambé*. *Déglacer* with white wine and reduce until almost all the liquid has evaporated. Add the tarragon, parsley, basil, *bouquet garni*, orange *zeste*, *pastis* and star *anise*. Transfer the ingredients into a large pot, cover with water, bring to a boil, skim the surface when necessary, and leave to simmer for 30 minutes. Blend or process, then pass through a fine sieve lined with cheesecloth. Bring to a boil again, skim, stir in the saffron, and check seasoning, adding salt and pepper to taste.

For the *aïoli*, mix the egg yolk and mustard together in a bowl. Slowly add the oils to the mixture, a little at a time, whisking vigorously until the mixture has the consistency of mayonnaise (a blender may be used for ease). Blend in the vinegar and garlic. Season with salt and pepper to taste.

For the *rouille*, cook the potatoes unpeeled in boiling salted water, then peel and mash. Hard boil the egg, peel, and separate the egg yolk. Mash the egg yolk and mix together with the mashed potato, chopped garlic, and hot pepper paste. Slowly add the oils a little at a time. Mix until you have a smooth mixture. Check seasoning, adding salt and pepper to taste.

To prepare the garnish, brush the rounds of bread with olive oil and bake in a hot oven until crispy and golden. Chop the parsley and grate the Parmesan.

Serve the soup hot, accompanied by *croûtons*, *aïoli*, *rouille*, grated Parmesan, and chopped parsley.

Chef's tip
This fish soup can easily be frozen. It is very versatile and can be served as an entrée or a main course. It is also ideal to use as a fish sauce.

La soupe de betterave rouge

BEETROOT SOUP

Inspired by a Borscht recipe supplied by an ex-student, Frédéric Rivière turned, with a few subtle changes, this Russian specialty into a soup with a distinct, contemporary French feel.

Soup
1 LB 2 OZ/510 G RAW BEETS
1¾ PT/1 LITER CHICKEN OR VEGETABLE STOCK
1 STALK OF CELERY

Garnish
4 NEW POTATOES
3½ TBSP/1¾ FL OZ/50 ML *CRÈME FRAÎCHE*
1 SPRIG OF CHERVIL

Seasoning
SALT
GROUND PEPPER
1 TBSP TABASCO SAUCE
1 TBSP WORCESTERSHIRE SAUCE

Preparation time: 1 hour 15 minutes
Cooking time: 45 minutes
Serves 4 people

Finely chop the beets and celery. Place the cut beets and celery into a pot and cover with the stock or broth. Season to taste with salt, pepper, Tabasco sauce and Worcestershire sauce. Simmer for up to 1 hour. When the beets are soft and thoroughly cooked, place in a blender or food processor and pass through a fine sieve.

To prepare the garnish, wash the potatoes and, leaving whole, place in cold salted water. Place on the heat and cook until tender. Drain and leave to cool. Cut in half, lengthways, and gently scoop out some of the soft potato pulp with a spoon or melon-baller, just enough to make a small well in the center of the potato. Set aside.

Reheat the soup and check the seasoning. Reheat the potatoes in a pan with a little water and olive oil. Remove from pan and place a spoonful of *crème fraîche* in the well in the center of the potato. Pour the hot soup into individual bowls and place a potato in the center. Sprinkle with chervil leaves.

Chef's tip
Canned beets in natural juice can be used to save time. The color of the final soup, however, will not be as striking as it is when using fresh beets. Made with vegetable stock, this recipe is a true vegetarian dish.

Les pâtés et les terrines

PÂTÉS AND TERRINES

When is a pâté a terrine and vice versa? The two terms have come to be virtually interchangeable today, but their origins are different. The former described a forcemeat baked in a pastry crust, whereas the latter was cooked in the eponymous earthenware container. Changes that have occurred in food fashion over the last three decades have given a completely new take on these two classic terms. Traditionally, meat pâtés and terrines were the privileged domain of charcutiers, pork butchers. Their recipes were substantial, high in protein and fat.

When chefs began applying their talents to this particular branch of the culinary art, they introduced lighter mixtures and mousses for minced and chopped pork. They also created "pressed" terrines, held together only by the cooked fish, meat or vegetables themselves. Modern terrines reflect the complete spectrum of creative cooking. They can be colorful, intensely flavored reflections of regional dishes or suave adaptations of classics, such as Frédéric Rivière's *Foie gras cuit en terrine* (page 28).

Le marbré de canard

MARBLED DUCK

"This dish is a fantastic example of how to serve different parts of the duck in one dish. The idea for this recipe was developed when I experimented with using different parts of an animal or bird to try and capture the many different flavors present in each part."

Frédéric Rivière

Duck
3½ oz/100 g fresh smoked duck breast
3½ oz/100 g *foie gras*/duck liver
7 oz/200 g duck leg/thigh *confit*
Olive oil

Garnish
3½ oz/100 g Golden Delicious apples
3½ oz/100 g pears
3½ oz/100 g grapes
1 tbsp butter

Sauce
7 tbsp/3½ fl oz/105 ml dry red wine
14 tbsp/7 fl oz/210 ml balsamic vinegar
¾ oz/20 g butter

Accompaniment
5¼ oz/150 g mache/lamb's-ear lettuce
1 sprig chervil
1 oz/30 g pine nuts
1 oz/30 g minced shallots

Seasoning
Salt
Ground pepper

Preparation time: 40 minutes (2 hours' refrigeration time)
Cooking time: 20 minutes
Serves 4 people

Cut the duck liver/*foie gras* into little cubes approximately ¼ in./7 mm square. Cut the smoked duck breast into fine strips. Very quickly *sauté* both the cubed *foie gras* and shredded smoked duck breast in a little olive oil. In a pan, warm the duck thighs in their own fat (when buying pre-prepared duck *confit*, it will come complete with the duck fat). Pull the meat from the bone, and shred into little pieces. The meat should be very tender and practically fall off the bone.

For the garnish, peel and core the apples and pears, and then slice thinly widthwise. *Sauté* together gently in butter, then drain the fruit on a paper towel.

To assemble, place four small bottomless stainless steel molds on a baking tray that has been covered with a sheet of aluminum foil. Line the sides with the apple slices and the bottom with the pear slices. Start by lining the bottom of the mold with a layer of grapes, then the duck *confit*, followed by the *foie gras* and a slice of duck breast. Cover with a pear slice. Place in the refrigerator until ready to serve (minimum 2 hours' refrigeration time before serving).

For the sauce, reduce the red wine and balsamic vinegar by three-quarters in a saucepan. Add the butter and allow it to melt.

Wash and prepare the salad. Mix in the pine nuts, minced shallots, chervil, salt and pepper. Pour a bit of the sauce over the top.

Carefully remove the mold, place the small individual duck terrine onto the center of a plate. Place the salad around the plate with a few drops of sauce. Serve with small triangles of toast.

Foie gras cuit en terrine

TERRINE OF FOIE GRAS

If you're French and throwing a party, it's likely that *foie gras* will figure somewhere on your menu. Along with champagne, it's treated as traditional festive food. Both geese and ducks, specially fattened to produce the characteristic large, buttery livers, are used for this delicacy, but duck *foie gras*, smaller and less expensive (though with more taste) tends to be more readily available. The southwest of France is the major *foie gras*-producing area, which specializes in using duck fat for many recipes – and has the lowest incidence of heart disease in the country.

Duck liver
14 OZ/400 G *FOIE GRAS*/DUCK LIVER

Seasoning
SALT
PEPPER
3½ TBSP/1¾ FL OZ/50 ML PORT

Garnish
7 OZ/200 G PEAR
7 OZ/200 G SMOKED DUCK BREAST
7 OZ/200 G CELERY
SLICES OF FARMHOUSE BREAD TO SERVE

Preparation time: 1 hour 30 minutes (refrigerate overnight)
Cooking time: 3 minutes
Serves 4 people

De-nerve the *foie gras*/duck liver by opening up the liver in the center with a very sharp knife. Take out the very fine nerve that will be visible in the center of the liver, approximately ¾ in./2 cm. From this, remove the second nerve. Place the de-nerved *foie gras* in a bowl of milk and ice cubes for at least 1 hour. Drain and pat dry. Spread the liver on a baking sheet and season with salt, pepper and port. Mold the liver into one small terrine mold. Bake in a preheated oven at 430°F/220°C for 3 minutes. Cool slightly, then cover the terrine with aluminum foil and weigh down with a smaller mold. Place in the refrigerator to set overnight before serving.

Before serving
Peel and cut the pear into small pieces and stew in a little water and fat from the liver for 30 minutes to make *compote*. Cut the celery into a fine *brunoise*, in a pan *sauté* quickly with a little duck fat. Cut the smoked duck breasts into rectangular strips.

Place a slice of *foie gras* in the center of a plate. Place three scoops of pear *compote* around the *foie gras* and sprinkle the celery and strips of duck breast over the top. Serve with lightly toasted triangles of farmhouse bread.

Chef's tip
As oven temperatures may vary, watch for fat that will rise from around the duck foie gras. *When the fat begins to bubble, immediately remove the terrine from the oven. The heat of the terrine will continue to cook the* foie gras *for several minutes once it has been removed from the oven.*

Terrine de légumes et de saumon, sauce printemps

VEGETABLE AND SALMON TERRINE WITH SPRING SAUCE

When Nouvelle Cuisine was at the height of its popularity, colorful, pretty terrines were the rage. Some were based on mousses, others on pressed vegetables, others still, like this dish, were bound together with a blend of eggs and cream known as *royale*.

Vegetables
3½ OZ/100 G BROCCOLI
3½ OZ/100 G SMALL PEAS
3½ OZ/100 G STRING BEANS
3½ OZ/100 G CARROTS
1 SMALL LEEK
1 TOMATO
1 RED PEPPER

Fish
2 SALMON FILLETS
7 OZ/200 G LARGE PRAWNS, PEELED
SALT AND GROUND BLACK PEPPER TO SEASON
3 EGGS
½ OZ/15 G TOMATO CONCENTRATE
13 TBSP/6½ FL OZ/200 ML CREAM
½ TSP/2 G SAFFRON
1 SPRIG FRESH THYME
SALT AND GROUND BLACK PEPPER TO SEASON

Spring sauce
7 OZ/200 G FRESH TOMATOES
4 BASIL LEAVES
1 TSP CHERVIL
1 TSP FRESH DILL
2 TBSP/1 FL OZ/30 ML BALSAMIC VINEGAR

Preparation time: 30 minutes
Cooking time: 30–50 minutes
Serves 4 people

Divide the broccoli into florets, shell the peas, top and tail the beans and chop the carrots into a *julienne*. Cut the tender white center part of the leek lengthwise. Peel and seed the tomatoes and pepper (see chef's tip) and cut into *julienne*. Steam all the vegetables together for a few minutes until tender.

Cut the salmon fillets into slices of ¼ in./7 mm. Season both the salmon and the peeled prawns with salt, pepper and fresh thyme. Steam the salmon and prawns together for approximately 10 seconds – just long enough to seal the flesh.

In a separate bowl, whisk together the eggs, tomato concentrate, cream, saffron, fresh thyme, salt and pepper.

This dish may be prepared in a single large terrine or in small individual molds. Oil the terrine (or molds) with olive oil and then line the bottom with half the sliced leek. Fill the terrine in layers, starting with broccoli, then the tomatoes, peas, a slice of fish, green beans, peppers, prawns and finally, carrots. Pour the egg mixture over and top with the remaining leeks.

Place the sheet of aluminum foil on the bottom of a roasting pan and put the terrine or molds in the pan. Fill the pan three-quarters full of water and cover the whole tray with another sheet of foil. Bake in a preheated oven at 300°F/150°C for 30–40 minutes for the smaller molds, and 40–50 minutes for a larger, single terrine.

To test if the terrine is cooked, place a knife in the center. If the knife comes out clean, the terrine is ready.

For the spring sauce, peel, seed, and chop the tomatoes and place in a blender with the remaining ingredients. Blend until smooth and check for seasoning.

Place a spoonful of the spring sauce on a plate and place the terrine on top. This dish can be served either hot or cold.

Chef's tip
To effectively peel tomatoes, score the skin lightly with a knife and plunge the tomatoes into a pan of boiling water for a few seconds. Take them from the hot water and put them directly into cold water. The skin will then peel away easily. To skin peppers, grill until the skins blacken. They will then peel easily.

Les entrées

APPETIZERS

Once upon a time, when dinners boasted as many as a dozen courses, the _entrée_ came after the _hors d'oeuvre_, soup and fish courses, but before the _relevé_ (what we might call a main dish), and various desserts. Eating has become more streamlined, the three-course meal a norm and its _entrée_ the conventional kicking off point.

Because its function has changed, so has its content. The looser English term "starter", or the more prevalent term "appetizer", may be less evocative, but it gives a better idea of the desire to do one's own thing, to be inventive – the aspiration of almost all modern chefs – which is the characteristic of current restaurant _entrées_.

At home, a simple _entrée_ might be a tomato salad or a _soupe aux légumes_. For the experienced cook, there are no boundaries beyond those of good taste. When choosing an appetizer from the recipes Frédéric Rivière has created in this chapter, imagine how it will balance with the other courses. Should it be hot or cold? Should it be based on fish, meat or vegetables? Will it whet the appetite for a substantial main course? Should the portions be generous or restrained?

Les petits farçis du moment au coulis de persil

MINI-STUFFED VEGETABLES WITH PARSLEY COULIS

This is another typical Provençal recipe, made from freshly picked baby vegetables garnered by Frédéric Rivière from Forville Market in Cannes. Once you have the knack of working with zucchini and cherry tomatoes, try building on your repertoire with eggplants, bell peppers, and artichoke bottoms or hollowed out new potatoes.

Stuffed cherry tomatoes
12 CHERRY TOMATOES
7 OZ/200 G MUSHROOMS
1¾ OZ/50 G SHALLOTS
½ GARLIC CLOVE
3½ TBSP/1¾ FL OZ/50 ML OLIVE OIL

Stuffed mini zucchini
4 MINI ZUCCHINI
3½ OZ/100 G RED PEPPERS
½ GARLIC CLOVE
3½ TSP/1¾ FL OZ/50 ML OLIVE OIL

Garnish
4 MINI ARTICHOKES
2¼ OZ/60 G ONION
2¼ OZ/60 G TOMATO
2¼ OZ/60 G CARROT
2¼ OZ/60 G CELERY
½ GARLIC CLOVE
4 CHERVIL LEAVES
4 BASIL FLOWERS
4 SPRIGS OF DILL
3½ TBSP/1¾ FL OZ/50 ML DRY WHITE WINE
JUICE OF ½ A LEMON

Seasoning
SALT
SECHUAN PEPPER
BLACK PEPPER

Coulis
3½ OZ/100 G FLAT/CHINESE PARSLEY
7 TBSP/3½ FL OZ/105 ML VEGETABLE STOCK

Chef's tip

To assist working with small tender vegetables, use a melon-baller to scoop out the flesh.

Preparation time: 1 hour 15 minutes
Cooking time: 25 minutes
Serves 4 people

To prepare the stuffed tomatoes, cut their tops off and scoop out the seeds. Next, clean and finely dice the mushrooms and chop the shallots and garlic. *Sauté* the mushrooms, shallots and garlic in olive oil for 20 minutes, then put in a blender and blend quickly. Take the tomatoes and stuff them with the mushroom mixture. Put their tops back on and put to one side.

Cook the mini zucchini in boiling salted water, then run them under cold water to retain their color. Slice the top one-quarter of the zucchini lengthwise and scoop out the flesh. Peel and cut the red peppers into little cubes, and cook covered for 20 minutes in some water, olive oil and garlic. When ready, fill the zucchini with the chopped red pepper and replace the top.

Next, take the artichokes and cut away the tough outer leaves. Remove the thistle and reserve in a bowl of water and lemon juice. Peel and cut the onion, tomato, carrot, celery and garlic into a *mirepoix* and sweat in olive oil for 5 minutes. Add the drained artichoke and cook for a further 3 minutes. *Déglacer* with white wine, reduce until all the liquid has evaporated, and then cover with water. Simmer on a low heat for 30 minutes. Check to see if the artichokes are cooked by inserting a knife into the middle of the artichoke between the heart and the stem. The knife should go in easily.

To make the parsley *coulis*, wash and pat dry the parsley, and cook for 30 seconds in the chicken stock. Blend or process and pass through a fine sieve.

Place the various vegetables in a star pattern on a plate. Decorate each with the fresh chervil, basil flowers and dill. Drizzle the sauce around.

Soufflé d'artichauts à la Provençale

PROVENÇAL ARTICHOKE SOUFFLÉ

Artichokes come in many sizes, shapes and colors, some large and bulbous, others tapering, some green, some tinted with violet, some smooth, some spiky. When choosing them, always pick them closed, firm and fresh. They should feel heavy in the hand.

Artichokes
4 ARTICHOKES
1 OZ/30 G CARROT
1 OZ/30 G LEEK
1 OZ/30 G ONION
1 OZ/30 G FENNEL
3½ TBSP/1¾ FL OZ/50 ML OLIVE OIL
1 GARLIC CLOVE
1 *BOUQUET GARNI*
3½ TBSP/1¾ FL OZ/50 ML DRY WHITE WINE
JUICE OF 1 LEMON

***Soufflé* base**
1 OZ/30 G FLOUR
1 OZ/30 G BUTTER
5 EGG WHITES

Sauce and seasoning
SALT
GROUND BLACK PEPPER
3½ TBSP/1¾ FL OZ/50 ML *TRUFFLE* OIL

Preparation time: 50 minutes
Cooking time: 20 minutes
Serves 4 people

Take the artichokes and cut away the tough outer leaves and thorny tops. Remove the thistle and reserve in a bowl of water and lemon juice to stop discoloration. Peel and cut the remaining vegetables into a *mirepoix* and along with the finely chopped garlic sweat in olive oil for 5 minutes. Add the drained artichoke and cook for a further 3 minutes. *Déglacer* with white wine, reduce until all the liquid has evaporated, and then cover with water and add the *bouquet garni*. Simmer for 30 minutes. When done, remove the artichokes and cut into quarters. Retain the liquid and other vegetables once the artichokes have been removed.

To make the *soufflé* base, melt the butter in a saucepan and stir in the flour. Cook for 2–3 minutes stirring continuously with a wooden spoon – you now have a *roux*. Remove from heat and whisk in half of the cooking liquid from the vegetables, stirring until smooth. Return the saucepan to the heat and boil for 2–3 minutes. Stir the artichokes into this *soufflé* mix.

Finally, beat the egg whites until stiff and fold carefully into the *soufflé* base. Pour into molds. If using large molds, bake in a preheated oven for 5 minutes at 430°F/220°C, then 390°F/200°C for 20 minutes. If the molds are smaller, bake for 3 minutes at 430°F/220°C, and 8 minutes at 390°F/200°C.

To make the sauce, blend or process the vegetables with the remaining cooking liquid and whisk in the *truffle* oil.

Serve the *soufflé* as soon as it comes from the oven; serve the sauce to one side in a sauceboat.

Chef's tip
To get the best results when beating together egg whites, take the eggs from the refrigerator at least 1 hour before using. If possible, use a copper bowl and make sure both the bowl and the whisk are free of oils.

Le croustillant de raviole du Roya à la brunoise de légumes

RAVIOLI FROM THE ROYA WITH FINELY DICED VEGETABLES

"This dish dates from the time when I worked at the late Fernand Point's famous restaurant at Vienne, La Pyramide. When I came to the Riviera I added a few touches to reflect the vegetables I was buying from the Roya valley behind Nice."

Frédéric Rivière

Brunoise
2¼ OZ/60 G TOMATOES
2¼ OZ/60 G YELLOW PEPPER
2¼ OZ/60 G ONION
2¼ OZ/60 G ZUCCHINI
2¼ OZ/60 G EGGPLANT
1 GARLIC CLOVE
1 SPRIG OF FRESH THYME
OLIVE OIL AS REQUIRED

Ravioli
14 OZ/400 G *RAVIOLI* (PRE-PREPARED VERY SMALL *RAVIOLI* WITH A BLUE CHEESE FILLING)
3½ TBSP/1¾ FL OZ/50 ML OLIVE OIL

Fennel *coulis*
2 SMALL FENNEL BULBS
3½ TBSP/1¾ FL OZ/50 ML OLIVE OIL
SALT
JUICE OF 1 LEMON
TEN FLAVORED PEPPER

Garnish
4 BASIL FLOWERS
4 SPRIGS OF DILL

Preparation time: 30 minutes
Cooking time: 15 minutes
Serves 4 people

Peel, seed, and cut the tomatoes into cubes. Peel and cut the yellow pepper and onion into a *brunoise* and *sauté* in olive oil, garlic and thyme, and season to taste. Repeat this process for the zucchini and eggplant. Once all the vegetables are cooked, mix together in the same pan.

Oil and line individual, non-stick, stainless steel bottomless molds approximately 1½–2½ in./4–6 cm in diameter with the pre-cooked *ravioli* and fill with the vegetable *brunoise*. Bake in a preheated oven at 390°F/200°C for 5 minutes.

For the fennel *coulis*, peel and cut the bulbs into large cubes and then cook in water with lemon juice and salt. Blend or process with a little olive oil, add a little water if the *coulis* is too thick. Season the *coulis* with salt and *ten flavored pepper*.

Remove the *ravioli* and vegetable filling from the mold and place in the center of a plate. Pour a thin stream of *coulis* around the *ravioli* and decorate with the fresh herbs.

Chef's tip
The ravioli *may be substituted with fresh, pre-cooked large flat noodles, or lasagne sheets.*

Le flan de légumes

VEGETABLE FLAN

In French cookery a flan is an open tart filled with fruit, cream, or a savory mixture. The word flan comes from the old French *flaon*, from the Latin *flado* (a flat cake). This very light dish is an excellent way to whet the appetite.

Vegetables

Carrot *purée*
7 OZ/200 G CARROTS
1 EGG YOLK
1 EGG WHITE
6 TBSP/3 FL OZ/90 ML HEAVY CREAM
¾ OZ/20 G BUTTER

Broccoli *purée*
7 OZ/200 G BROCCOLI
1 EGG YOLK
1 EGG WHITE BEATEN
5 TBSP/2¾ FL OZ/80 ML HEAVY CREAM

Spinach
8 SPINACH LEAVES
3½ TBSP/1¾ FL OZ/50 ML OLIVE OIL

Biscuits
2¼ OZ/60 G FLOUR
2¼ OZ/60 G EGG WHITES
1 OZ/30 G BUTTER
½ OZ/15 G SESAME SEEDS

Seasoning and garnish
SALT
WHITE PEPPER
SEA SALT
4 EDIBLE FLOWERS
3½ TBSP/1¾ FL OZ/50 ML *TRUFFLE* OIL

Preparation time: 20 minute
Cooking time: 35 minutes
Serves 4 people

Peel and slice the carrots. Boil in water, with a little salt, pepper and butter, until tender. Drain and return the carrots to the saucepan over a low heat to remove any excess moisture. Leave to cool slightly and then blend or process until smooth. Put these *puréed* carrots in a bowl and stir in the egg yolk, beaten egg white and the cream. Season with salt and pepper to taste.

Cook the broccoli in boiling salted water until tender. Run under cold water to retain the color, pat dry and leave to cool slightly. Blend or process with the egg yolk, cream, salt and pepper, and then stir in the beaten egg white.

Wash the spinach leaves and remove the tough central stems. Blanch in boiling water for a few seconds, drain, and run under cold water. Squeeze any excess water from the leaves.

Take four *ramekins* and line the insides with the spinach. Fill halfway with the carrot *purée*. Pour the broccoli *purée* on top to fill. Place in a *bain-marie* and cook in the oven, covered with aluminum foil, at 350°F/180°C for 30 minutes.

While this is cooking, prepare the biscuits by mixing all the ingredients together in order. Take a non-stick baking sheet and spread out the mixture to make eight circles. Bake in a preheated oven at 355°F/180°C for 5 minutes or until lightly colored. Wait until completely cooled to remove from the baking sheet.

Remove the flan from the molds and put in the center of a plate. Place two biscuits on top, decorate with edible flowers, and sprinkle some *truffle* oil around the plate.

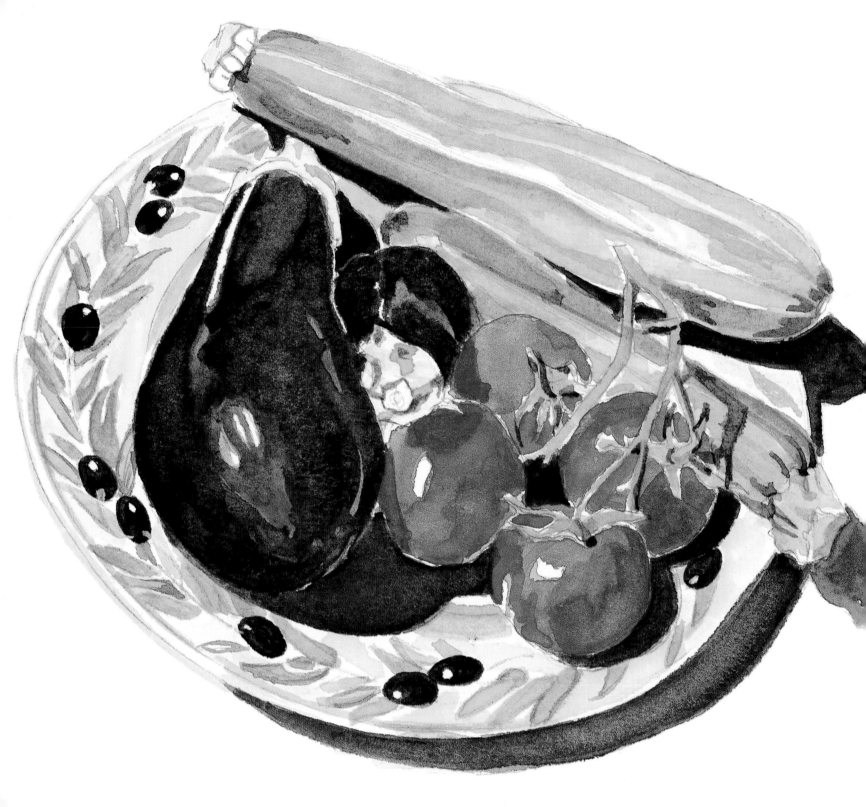

Légumes confits et sèches en terrine

DRIED VEGETABLE CONFIT IN A TERRINE

This terrine is derived from a traditional Provençal dish: *Le Tian*, which is a type of vegetable "cake". It is perfectly suited for a light summer lunch with a glass of chilled *rosé* wine.

Terrine
4 TOMATOES
12 GARLIC CLOVES
2 EGGPLANTS
2 ZUCCHINI
6½ TBSP/3½ FL OZ/105 ML OLIVE OIL
3½ TBSP/1¾ FL OZ/50 ML WATER
1 SPRIG FRESH THYME
1 BAY LEAF
8 PITTED BLACK OLIVES
4 BASIL LEAVES

Herb *coulis*
3½ OZ/100 G FRESH HERBS (DILL, CHIVE, PARSLEY AND BASIL)
4 TBSP/2 FL OZ/60 ML VEGETABLE STOCK

Seasoning
FINE SALT
TEN FLAVORED PEPPER
SECHUAN OR RED CHILLI POWDER
SUGAR

Preparation time: 1 hour
Cooking time: 35 minutes
Serves 4 people

Peel, quarter and remove the seeds from the tomatoes and place them on a baking sheet. Season with fine salt, Sechuan pepper and sugar and dry in the oven set at 300°F/150°C. Cover the garlic (still in husks) in olive oil and add the *ten flavored pepper*, sprig of thyme and bay leaf. Cook for 30 minutes and then remove the pulp and reserve the pulp. Cut the eggplants into ¾ in./2 cm pieces and place them on a baking sheet. Season with fine salt, Sechuan pepper and olive oil. Bake in the oven at 300°F/150°C for 30 minutes. Place them in a saucepan with olive oil and a little water. Season with salt and *ten flavored pepper* and cook until soft.

For individual portions, use a mold that is approximately 2½ in./6 cm in diameter and 1½ in./4 cm in height. Place the vegetables in layers in the following order: eggplant, zucchini, garlic, chopped basil and olives. Apply some pressure after each layer and heat lightly before serving.

For the herb *coulis*, wash and remove the herbs from their stems. Bring the vegetable stock to a boil and let the herbs infuse for 5 minutes then remove and reserve. Bring the stock back to a boil, add the herbs, bring back to a boil and immediately remove them from the heat and mix in a food processor or blender. Heat slightly to serve.

Pour the *coulis* onto the plate. Turn out the terrine in the center, sprinkle with herbs and decorate with the herb *coulis*.

La roulade du mas des oliviers

LE MAS DES OLIVIERS SALMON ROLL

"I've christened this recipe after the Rhode School of Cuisine villa. The name translates loosely as 'Olive Tree Farm' and is symbolic of the Provençal countryside. The combination of smoked salmon and artichoke, surprising in itself, is perfectly adapted to entertaining on a terrace on a balmy summer evening."

Frédéric Rivière

Artichoke *purée*
4 ARTICHOKES
3½ TBSP/1¾ FL OZ/50 ML CREAM
SALT
GROUND PEPPER

Pesto
3 GARLIC CLOVES, CRUSHED
6½ TBSP/3¼ FL OZ/100 ML OLIVE OIL
5¼ OZ/150 G FRESH BASIL LEAVES
2 TBSP PINE NUTS

Fish
14 OZ/400 G SMOKED SALMON

Garnish
2 TOMATOES
4 BASIL LEAVES (WITH FLOWERS IF POSSIBLE)

Preparation time: 35 minutes
Cooking time: 30 minutes
Serves 4 people

To make the artichoke *purée*, remove the stems from the artichokes and cook in boiling salted water until tender. Scrape the flesh from the leaves and coarsely chop the hearts after removing the thistles. Place in a blender, with the cream and seasoning, and blend until smooth.

To make the pesto, use a blender or mortar and pestle to combine together the basil, garlic, pine nuts and olive oil. Season to taste.

Cut the salmon into twelve thin slices, approximately 1½ in./4 cm in width, 3 in./8 cm long. Place a spoonful of the artichoke *purée* on each slice and roll up, securing the ends by squashing the edges together. The smoked salmon should be rather oily and so will easily stick together.

Peel, seed, and chop the tomato flesh into cubes.

Arrange two salmon rolls on each serving plate with a spoonful of the pesto and chopped tomatoes. Garnish with shredded basil leaves.

Chef's tip
The salmon rolls can also be cut into bite-sized pieces and served as canapés.

Composition de la mer en marinade

A MEDLEY OF MARINATED FISH

Cooking without heat? Yes, it is possible. By marinating fish in citrus juices or vinegars, the fish is effectively "cooked". Once prepared, the fish will keep perfectly fresh in the fridge for two to three days.

Salmon
7 OZ/200 G SALMON
2 STEMS FRESH CILANTRO (CORIANDER LEAVES)
3½ TBSP/1¾ FL OZ/50 ML FIG VINEGAR
6½ TBSP/3½ FL OZ/105 ML DILL OIL
JUICE OF 1 LEMON
GREEN PEPPERCORNS
SEA SALT

Salmon garnish
3½ OZ/100 G MUSHROOMS
1¾ OZ/50 G RED LEAF LETTUCE

Scorpion fish
7 OZ/200 G SCORPION FISH OR TURBOT
1 SPRIG OF FRESH DILL
3½ TBSP/1¾ FL OZ/50 ML BALSAMIC VINEGAR
JUICE OF 1 LEMON
SECHUAN PEPPER
6½ TBSP/3½ FL OZ/105 ML SEA SALT

Scorpion fish garnish
3½ OZ/100 G CUCUMBERS
1¾ OZ/50 G ARUGULA/*ROCKET*

Shrimp
7 OZ/200 G SHRIMP
FRESH CHIVES
6½ TBSP/3½ FL OZ/105 ML FENNEL OIL
FIVE FLAVORED PEPPER
JUICE OF 1 LEMON
3½ OZ/100 G TOMATOES
SEA SALT

Shrimp garnish
3½ OZ/100 G TOMATOES
1¾ OZ/50 G MACHE/LAMB'S-EAR LETTUCE

Preparation time: 30 minutes
Serves 4 people

Proceed in the same manner for all three of the fish.

Bone the fish and cut into thin slices. Peel the shrimp. Chop the herbs and mix together with all the remaining ingredients, apart from the oils. Place each fish into its marinade and leave for 5 minutes. The acidity of the lemon juice will cook the fish. You should see the fish slowly turning a lighter color. Next, add the oil. This will stop the fish cooking. For the garnishes, thinly slice the mushrooms, peel and cut the cucumbers into small cubes, peel, seed and cube the tomatoes, and wash the lettuces.

Using cookie cutters as a mold, make three circles on a plate; place a layer of vegetables (the mushrooms, cucumbers and tomatoes) in each mold, followed by a spoonful of relevant marinated fish. Decorate each with the appropriate lettuce.

Petits gris en persillade sur un tapis de champignons des bois

"PETITS GRIS" ESCARGOTS WITH PARSLEY BUTTER
AND WILD MUSHROOMS

Eating snails is part of the Latin culinary culture, espoused by French, Italians and Spanish alike. Although different kinds vary in size, their taste and texture (quite chewy) is similar. They have a special affinity with a blend of parsley, garlic and butter.

Snails
8 SNAILS, FRESH IF AVAILABLE

Sauce
3½ OZ/100 G PARSLEY
7 OZ/200 G BUTTER
2 GARLIC CLOVES
1¾ OZ/50 G SHALLOTS
JUICE OF 1 LEMON

Mushrooms
10½ OZ/300 G WILD MUSHROOMS
3½ TBSP/1¾ FL OZ/50 ML SESAME OIL

Seasoning
SALT
BLACK PEPPER

Preparation time: 30 minutes
Cooking time: 7–10 minutes
Serves 4 people

Wash and drain the snails and pat dry. In a bowl, mix together the parsley, butter and crushed garlic, shallots and lemon juice and season with salt and pepper.

Clean the mushrooms and remove any excess moisture by tossing them in a very hot pan. *Sauté* in sesame oil. Season and set aside.

Place the mushrooms in individual ovenproof serving dishes, and cover with snails and garlic parsley butter sauce. Bake in a preheated oven at 390°F/200°C for 7–10 minutes.

Chef's tip
If possible, when buying snails for this dish, look for petits-gris *on the label – these are a small and delicate variety, as opposed to the large, sometimes tough, variety known as* bourgogne.

Les mini-crêpes à la coriandre, fourées au fromage de chèvre frais et fruits secs

MINI CILANTRO CRÊPES FILLED WITH GOAT CHEESE AND DRIED FRUIT

"The idea for this recipe came from a trip I made to Texas in 1997. Cilantro is used frequently in Texan cooking which tends to have a strong Mexican influence. It was a herb I had not used much previous to my visit. This recipe is a great mix of the two cuisines, French *crêpes* with goat cheese, with the addition of cilantro as the Mexican influence."

Frédéric Rivière

Crêpes
2¼ oz/60 g FRESH CILANTRO (CORIANDER LEAVES)
13 TBSP/6¾ FL OZ/200 ML MILK
3½ TBSP/1¾ FL OZ/50 ML BEER
2 EGGS
4½ OZ/130 G FLOUR
1 OZ/30 G BUTTER
SALT
BLACK PEPPER

Goat cheese
4 SLICES OF FRESH GOAT CHEESE
1 OZ/30 G PINE NUTS
1 OZ/30 G WALNUTS
1 OZ/30 G RAISINS

Seasoning
SALT
WHITE PEPPER
PAPRIKA

Balsamic concentrate sauce
3½ OZ/100 G SUGAR
2 TBSP/1 FL OZ/30 ML WATER
3½ TBSP/1¾ FL OZ/50 ML WATER
HAZELNUT OIL TO SERVE
6½ TBSP/3¾ FL OZ/105 ML BALSAMIC VINEGAR

Preparation time: 1 hour 15 minutes
Cooking time: 30 minutes
Serves 4 people

For the *crêpes*, finely chop the cilantro and mix in a bowl with the milk, beer, eggs, salt and pepper. Add the sifted flour and stir with a wooden spoon until smooth. Set aside for 1 hour. To cook, lightly butter a small skillet and pour in a small amount of the *crêpe* mixture. Cook for approximately 3 minutes, flip, and cook for 1 more minute.

For the goat cheese, mix together all the ingredients in a bowl and season with salt and paprika.

For the sauce, place the sugar in a pan; add just enough water so that it is fully absorbed by the sugar. Cook slowly over a low heat until it becomes a golden brown. Wipe the sides of the pan with a knife to remove any pieces of sugar that may have crystallized on the edges. You should now have a thick caramel in the pan. *Déglacer* with 3½ tablespoons of water or half the quantity of caramel. At the same time, in another pan, reduce the balsamic vinegar by a quarter. Finally mix together the caramel and balsamic vinegar until you have a taste that is not too sweet and not too bitter. The balsamic concentrate will keep well in a bottle and can be used on many dishes as a decoration.

Place a spoonful of the goat cheese mixture in the center of each *crêpe* and roll up. On a lightly oiled baking tray, heat the *crêpes* in a warm oven. Place a *crêpe* in the center of a plate and pour the balsamic concentrate around the plate along with a splash of hazelnut oil.

Chef's tip
Choose a young goat cheese when making this dish – the cheese will melt more quickly and be less stringy than a more mature cheese.

Étuvée de fenouil et de tomates à la Provençale

BRAISED FENNEL AND TOMATO PROVENÇAL

Provence in general and the old Comté de Nice in particular are rich in vegetable dishes. Many are of Ligurian origin. The border between France and the old kingdom of Savoy changed often throughout history and the culinary practises reflect both sides of it. This recipe, quintessentially Mediterranean, could equally well have derived from Genoa or San Remo.

Vegetables
4 FENNEL BULBS
4 TOMATOES
3½ OZ/100 G BACON, CHOPPED
2¼ OZ/60 G ONIONS
2¼ OZ/60 G LEEKS
2¼ OZ/60 G CARROTS
3 BUTTON MUSHROOMS
2 GARLIC CLOVES
½ A LEMON

Seasoning
1 *BOUQUET GARNI*
SALT
FRESHLY GROUND BLACK PEPPER
OLIVE OIL
FRESH BASIL LEAVES

Garnish
BASIL FLOWERS
FRESH BASIL LEAVES

Preparation time: 45 minutes
Cooking time: 25 minutes
Serves 4 people

Peel the fennel bulbs and cut into quarters. Store in a bowl of water with a squeeze of lemon juice until required. Peel, seed, and cut the tomatoes into quarters. Peel and finely chop the leek, onion, carrot, mushroom, and garlic. In a saucepan over medium heat, sweat the chopped vegetables, fennel, and tomatoes in olive oil until all the liquid has evaporated. Add enough water to cover the contents of the saucepan, and then add the chopped bacon, *bouquet garni* and seasoning. Cover the pan and simmer for 30 minutes on low heat.

Serve in a soup bowl with the juices poured on top and sprinkle with shredded basil for decoration. This dish may be served hot or cold.

Chef's tip
To test if vegetables such as fennel or artichokes are cooked, push a knife into the center of the vegetable. When the knife comes out easily, the vegetable is cooked.

Les crustacés

SHELLFISH

France's coastal regions are a shellfish lover's paradise. Stop by the fish market in any port and you will see three or four varieties of shrimp wriggling in boxes, live lobsters and crabs, langoustines, scallops, mussels, oysters, clams and, probably, half a dozen other sorts of mollusks or crustaceans you've never seen before.

In a restaurant or brasserie, you may order the pick of the catch, dished up on crushed ice as a *plateau de fruits de mer*. You'll eat this with your fingers, drink Muscadet, Pouilly Fumé or Chablis and think you've gone to heaven.

There is only one key to shellfish: freshness. If it's not alive (with the exception of the best frozen langoustines) before you cook it, it's not worth eating … and the only rule of cooking shellfish is: don't overcook it. Mussels shrivel, scallops turn rubbery, and crab dries out.

Le tian de courgettes aux fruits de mer

SCALLOPS, LOBSTER AND SHRIMP WITH A ZUCCHINI CROWN

In regional cookery, a *tian* was an earthenware dish used for baking, especially for combinations of layered vegetables. Its name has been applied by chefs to modern dishes assembled in hoops that have evolved from earlier *tian* recipes.

Shellfish
4 SCALLOPS
4 SPINY LOBSTERS
7 OZ/200 G SHRIMPS
3½ TBSP/1¾ FL OZ/50 ML OLIVE OIL
SALT
GROUND BLACK PEPPER

Crown
12 TOMATO SLICES
3½ OZ/100 G EGGPLANT
2 ZUCCHINI
3½ TBSP/1¾ FL OZ/50 ML OLIVE OIL

Vinaigrette
6½ TBSP/3½ FL OZ/105 ML OLIVE OIL
3½ TBSP/1¾ FL OZ/50 ML WINE VINEGAR
1 SPRIG OF FRESH DILL

Garnish
SELECTION OF FRESH HERBS

Preparation time: 30 minutes
Cooking time: 15 minutes
Serves 4 people

Cut out the nerve of the scallop. Peel and clean the spiny lobsters and shrimp. Season and *sauté* in olive oil.

To prepare the crown, cook the sliced tomatoes and eggplant on a seasoned and oiled baking sheet. Cut the zucchini lengthwise into thin slices and blanch for a few seconds in boiling water. Run the eggplant under cold water and drain. Line the zucchini along the sides of four individual small oiled, bottomless, stainless steel ring molds, approximately 3 in./8 cm in diameter. Fill with layers of tomato, eggplant and shellfish. Bake in a preheated oven at 350°F/180°C for 5 minutes.

For the vinaigrette, heat the oil, vinegar, salt and pepper together. Just before serving, add fresh dill.

Remove the crown from the mold onto the center of a plate. Pour the vinaigrette around and decorate with fresh herbs.

Rouleaux de homard aux fevettes et jus de poulet

CHINESE SPRING ROLL WITH LOBSTER, BROAD BEANS AND A CHICKEN JUS

French chefs came late to fusion cooking and have always shown great discretion when adapting ingredients borrowed from other cultures. Here, spring roll wrappers, poached rather than fried are a nod, but no more, to Cantonese cuisine.

Lobster
2 LOBSTERS
2¼ OZ/60 G CARROT
2¼ OZ/60 G ONION
1 FINELY CHOPPED GARLIC CLOVE
3½ TBSP/1¾ FL OZ/50 ML DRY WHITE WINE
1 *BOUQUET GARNI*
4 SHEETS CHINESE *RAVIOLI*/SPRING ROLL WRAPPERS
3½ PT/2 LITERS WATER

Chicken sauce
3½ TBSP/1¾ FL OZ/50 ML *TRUFFLE* OIL
13 TBSP/6½ FL OZ/195 ML CHICKEN STOCK

Garnish
7 OZ/200 G BABY LIMA BEANS

Seasoning
SALT
SECHUAN PEPPER
SEA SALT
1 GARLIC CLOVE

Preparation time: 45 minutes
Cooking time: 25 minutes
Serves 4 people

To prepare the lobster, peel and cut the onion and carrot into a *mirepoix*. Make a *court-bouillon* by putting together the onion, garlic, carrot, white wine and *bouquet garni*. Season with sea salt and garlic. Cover with 3½ pt/2 liters of water and bring to a boil for 20 minutes. Plunge the live lobsters into the *court-bouillon* and cook for 6 minutes, then drain. Shell the lobster and cut the tail into medallions. With a cookie cutter, cut out 16 circles of Chinese *ravioli*. Just before serving, poach the *ravioli* in simmering salted water for 30 seconds and drain.

For the chicken sauce, reduce the chicken stock, reserving some for the garnish. Whisk in the *truffle* oil when ready to serve.

Prepare the garnish by cooking the baby lima beans in boiling salted water, then running under cold water and drain. Just before serving, reheat in some of the chicken stock.

Layer the *ravioli* and lobster medallions. Spread the baby lima beans around the plate and pour over the sauce.

Mousse de langoustines à la trilogie de poireaux

LANGOUSTINE MOUSSE WITH THREE KINDS OF LEEKS

To a good cook, a leek is one of the key vegetables, not just an ingredient to add to the soup. Allowed to grow, it can weigh over a pound, but special mini-varieties are harvested, pencil thin. Some recipes use only the white root, others the whole vegetable; and the green tops make an ideal wrapper for a *bouquet garni*. Their sweet onion-like taste makes them an ideal accompaniment for shellfish.

Mousse
¾ OZ/20 G SHALLOTS
1 GARLIC CLOVE
3½ TBSP/1¾ FL OZ/50 ML OLIVE OIL
1 SPRIG FRESH THYME
14 OZ/400 G SCAMPI
SALT AND PEPPER TO SEASON
3½ TBSP/1¾ FL OZ/50 ML DRY VERMOUTH
6½ TBSP/3½ FL OZ/100 ML CREAM
2 EGG WHITES
12 SPINACH LEAVES

Stewed leeks
7 OZ/200 G LEEK WHITES
3½ TBSP/1¾ FL OZ/50 ML OLIVE OIL
3½ TBSP/1¾ FL OZ/50 ML DRY WHITE WINE
1 SPRIG FRESH THYME
1 CRUSHED GARLIC CLOVE

Puréed leeks
7 OZ/200 G LEEKS (WHITE PART)
3½ OZ/100 G POTATO
1 CRUSHED GARLIC CLOVE

Fried leeks
7 OZ/200 G LEEKS (WHITE PART)
13 TBSP/6¾ FL OZ/200 ML SUNFLOWER OIL
FOR FRYING

Sauce
2½ OZ/60 G TOMATO
2½ OZ/60 G LEMON
2½ OZ/60 G BLACK OLIVES
6½ TBSP/3½ FL OZ/105 ML OLIVE OIL
2 TBSP/1 FL OZ/30 ML BALSAMIC VINEGAR

Seasoning
SALT
SECHUAN PEPPER
SEA SALT
6–8 BASIL LEAVES

Preparation time: 1 hour
Cooking time: 25 minutes
Serves 4 people

To prepare the mousse, sweat the minced shallots, garlic and sprig of thyme in olive oil. Add the scampi, salt, pepper and thyme, and continue to cook for 1 minute. *Déglacer* with dry vermouth. Blend or process and set aside to cool. Fold the whipped cream and beaten egg white into the mixture. Blanch the spinach leaves for 5 seconds in boiling water, run under cold water and pat dry. Place a spoonful of mousse on each leaf. Close the leaf to form a small parcel and roll it in plastic wrap and twist ends to close. Steam the spinach parcels for 5–10 minutes, remove from the steamer, and remove the plastic wrap. Brush with olive oil just before serving.

For the stewed leeks, clean and slice the leeks into ½ in./1.5 cm rounds. Place the leeks in a large pot with white wine, olive oil, water and seasoning. Cook covered over a low heat for 25 minutes.

For the *puréed* leeks, peel the potatoes and wash the leeks. Chop coarsely and cook with garlic in salted water for 30 minutes. Blend or process into a smooth *purée* and set aside.

To prepare the fried leeks, wash and cut the leeks into a fine *julienne*. Pat dry. Deep fry in oil at 355°F/180°C until lightly golden. Drain on a paper towel.

For the sauce, peel, seed and cut the tomatoes into small cubes. Peel the lemon and cut out quarters in between the membrane, then cut into cubes. Pit the olives and cut into fine slivers. Mix the three ingredients together in a pan with the oil and vinegar. Reheat just before serving and season with salt and Sechuan pepper. Add the basil just before serving.

Arrange the three different leeks on a plate, placing a parcel of mousse on top. Pour the sauce around.

Chef's tip
As an alternative to the individual parcels, a ramekin lined with the spinach leaf and covered with aluminum foil, can be cooked in the oven at 355°F/180°C or steamed in a pan.

Le poisson

FISH

Until quite recently, fish cookery was intimately linked to making sauces and there was a hierarchy of desirable fish: sole, turbot and salmon being the most noble. As a result, the prestigious dishes were those like *filets de sole normande*, which combined a buttery, creamy reduction sauce, a fillet of Dover sole and a shellfish garnish.

Delicious as classic recipes of that type are, they don't represent contemporary fish cookery. First of all, the prejudice in favor of a handful of very expensive species no longer exists. Cod, mackerel, red mullet, monkfish and bass (*loup de mer*) are as highly regarded as salmon once was.

The trend away from rich coating sauces means that fish dishes, grilled, steamed or baked, both as fillets and on the bone are more exciting and less predictable. They are also less forgiving. It's impossible to disguise any lack of freshness.

The best fish cookery starts with careful shopping, buying only the brightest eyed, firmest specimens in the market. Modern fish farming means that certain species (gilt bream, bass, turbot, salmon) are readily available, no longer the exclusive preserve of restaurants. Fresh fish, of good quality, is easy to locate. At the same time, this puts a special value on wild or line caught fish, perceived by gourmets to have better texture and taste.

Rouleaux de lotte aux cèpes cuit en croûte de sel

MONKFISH AND PORCINI BAKED IN A SALT CRUST

Baking fish or even meat in salt is a practice going back over a century. Bass done this way is a specialty of Seville in Spain, and ribs of beef baked in salt belong to the répertoire of great French provincial dishes. Surprisingly, the monkfish doesn't taste any saltier than if it had been seasoned normally, but a coarse sea salt, such as the *sel gris* from Guérande, gives the best results.

Fish
3 OZ/85 G MONKFISH FILLET
7 OZ/200 G PORCINI MUSHROOMS
3½ TBSP/1¾ FL OZ/50 ML OLIVE OIL
1 CLOVE OF GARLIC
3½ TBSP/1¾ FL OZ/50 ML DRY VERMOUTH
SALT AND GROUND BLACK PEPPER TO SEASON

Crust
2½ LB/1 KG SEA SALT
5 EGG WHITES
¾ OZ/20 G *HERBS DE PROVENCE*
2¼ OZ/60 G FLOUR

Garnish
10½ OZ/300 G FINGERLING POTATOES
1¾ OZ/50 G CREAM
3½ TBSP/1¾ FL OZ/50 ML *TRUFFLE* OIL

Preparation time: 1 hour
Cooking time: 30 minutes
Serves 4 people

Clean and fillet the fish. Open the fish fillet by cutting it with a knife, lay the fillet flat as much as possible. Slice the porcini mushrooms and *sauté* in olive oil and season with a little finely chopped garlic, dry vermouth, salt and pepper. Place the mushrooms on the flattened fish fillet and roll it into a cylinder. Tie with string at both ends. In a pan, brown the fish very quickly in hot olive oil; then place the fish roll on a piece of parchment paper. Roll the fish in the parchment paper, tucking in the ends to form a parcel.

For the salt crust, mix together the salt, egg whites, flour and herbs. Take the rolled fish fillets and cover them with the salt mixture. Transfer to a baking tray and bake in a preheated oven at 390°F/200°C for 10 minutes.

For the garnish, peel and wash the potatoes, place them in a pot of cold water and cook until tender. Drain and dry the potatoes in a hot pan. Mash the potatoes, adding the cream and *truffle* oil.

Break the salt crust in front of the dinner guest. Remove from the wax paper, reserving the cooking juices. Slice the roll into 1 in./2.5 cm portions. Arrange the slices on a plate and add a scoop of potato. Pour over the cooking juices.

Chef's tip
If you are preparing this dish in advance and it has been in the fridge for some time, cook for 15–20 minutes in the oven at 390°F/200°C.

Bouillabaisse

BOUILLABAISSE

For such a famous dish, it's to be expected that there's plenty of argument as to how it evolved and how it should be prepared. Marseillais are renowned for their argumentative nature. Still, there is general agreement that the dish derives from *bouille* (boil – that is bring the pot to a boil) and *baisse* (lower – that is turn down the heat). Rockfish (see *Soupe de Poisson* recipe, page 23) form the base of this soup-stew, but it should also contain a variety of white fish too, enough to make a meal.

Fish (see Chef's tip)
2 × 3½ OZ/100 G RASCASSE/ROCK FISH
1 × 15 OZ/425 G TURBOT
2 LARGE RED MULLET (APPROXIMATELY
7 OZ/200–250 G)
1 × 7 OZ/200 G MONKFISH
1 × 7 OZ/200 G SAINT-PIERRE/JOHN DORY
4 SCAMPI

Fish soup
(SEE RECIPE FOR PROVENÇAL FISH SOUP, P. 23)
MAKE ENOUGH SOUP FOR FOUR PEOPLE PLUS AN
ADDITIONAL 2½ CUPS FOR INGREDIENTS THAT FOLLOW

Saffron potatoes
3 MEDIUM POTATOES
8 TBSP/4 FL OZ/120 ML FISH SOUP
8 TBSP/4 FL OZ/120 ML WATER
2 G SAFFRON
SEA SALT TO SEASON

Vegetables
1 CARROT
1 LEEK
2 CUPS FISH SOUP

To serve
AÏOLI (SEE PROVENÇAL FISH SOUP, P. 23)
ROUILLE (SEE PROVENÇAL FISH SOUP, P. 23)
GRATED PARMESAN CHEESE
1 BAGUETTE
OLIVE OIL FOR SPRAYING

Seasoning
SEA SALT
FRESHLY GROUND BLACK PEPPER
½ TSP/2 G SAFFRON
2¼ OZ/60 G CHOPPED PARSLEY

Preparation time: 1 hour 30 minutes
Cooking time: 30 minutes
Serves 4 people

For the saffron potatoes, wash and peel the potatoes and cut into slices of ⅛ in./2–3 mm thick. Place the potatoes into a large pot with the fish soup and water (there should be just enough liquid to cover the potatoes, add more if necessary). Add the saffron and season with sea salt. Cook the potatoes for approximately 20 minutes, or until the potatoes are cooked through but firm.

For the vegetables, *julienne* carrot and leek into ½ in./6–7 mm slices. Simmer the carrot separately in small pots with approximately 1 cup/240 ml each of fish soup.

Just prior to serving, slice the baguette into small rounds, spray or brush with olive oil and sprinkle with grated Parmesan cheese. Place the slices on a baking tray and bake for approximately 7–10 minutes until crispy and golden.

Bring the remainder of the fish soup to a simmer. Meanwhile, season the fish with salt and pepper. Poach the portions in the fish soup for approximately 3–5 minutes, depending on the size of the fish. Serve in large soup bowls with a layer of saffron potatoes on the bottom, followed by a piece of each of the fish, scampi, the carrot and leek (without the liquid) and a ladle of fish soup on the top. Season with parsley, saffron, salt and pepper. The rest of the soup should be left in the center of the table so that guests can replenish and heat the fish throughout the course. Serve with the *croûtons* and the side dishes of Parmesan, *aïoli* and *rouille*.

Chef's tip
Choose at least four varieties of fish – the greater the variety of fish, the more intense the flavor will be. However, oily fish such as salmon, herring or sardines are not suitable. Retain the soup liquid used for carrot and leek for future use.

Le dos de saumon sauce morilles

FILLET OF SALMON WITH MOREL SAUCE

Morels are a rare and expensive spring mushroom looking somewhat like a conical honeycomb. If you can't buy them fresh, reconstituted dried morels make a reasonable substitute.

Salmon
1 LB 5 OZ/600 G FILLET OF SALMON
2 SPRIGS OF PARSLEY
3½ TBSP/1¾ FL OZ/50 ML OLIVE OIL
1 GARLIC CLOVE

Garnish
4 ARTICHOKES
JUICE OF ½ A LEMON
3½ TBSP/1¾ FL OZ/50 ML OLIVE OIL
1 SPRIG OF FRESH THYME
½ GARLIC CLOVE
SALT AND GROUND BLACK PEPPER TO SEASON
6½ OZ/200 G *TROMPETTE/TRUMPET* MUSHROOMS
6½ OZ/200 G PEAS

Sauce
5 OZ/150 G MOREL MUSHROOMS
1¾ OZ/50 G BUTTER
1¾ OZ/50 G SHALLOTS
3½ TBSP/1¾ FL OZ/50 ML *COGNAC*
12 TBSP/6 FL OZ/180 ML CHICKEN STOCK
6 TBSP/3 FL OZ/90 ML CREAM

Preparation time: 45 minutes
Cooking time: 20 minutes
Serves 4 people

Clean, bone and portion the salmon. Make small incisions in the fish and insert the parsley. Cook the fish fillet, skin side only in olive oil and finely chopped garlic clove.

For the garnish, trim the artichoke and remove the heart. Sprinkle with lemon juice and slice very finely. *Sauté* the artichokes in olive oil and season with finely chopped garlic, thyme, salt and pepper. Set aside until needed.

Clean and dry the *trompette* mushrooms. *Sauté* in olive oil. Season and set aside. Cook the peas in boiling salted water. Reheat the peas just before serving in 3½ tbsp/1¾ fl oz/50 ml of water and olive oil.

For the sauce, sweat the minced shallots in butter, add three-quarters of the morel mushrooms, and cook for 4–5 minutes. *Flambé* with *Cognac* and cover with chicken stock. Heat for another 5 minutes, remove from the heat, add the cream, and blend or process the sauce. Check the seasoning and consistency (it should not be too thick). Reheat the remaining whole morel mushrooms in the sauce just before serving.

Spoon a portion of the sauce into the center of your serving plate and arrange the vegetables around the plate. Place the salmon skin-side-up in the center of the plate and decorate with a few of the whole morel mushrooms.

Chef's tip
If you prefer a milder tasting sauce, try using button, portobello or oyster mushrooms.

Les rougets aux trois purées

SAUTÉED RED MULLET WITH CELERY, ONION AND BROCCOLI PURÉES

The red mullet of the Mediterranean are small compared to their Atlantic cousins and it's usual to serve a couple as a portion. They have a nickname *bécasse de mer*, sea woodcock, because their "inner plumbing" is edible like the game bird's. The liver is, in fact, a delicacy. If you're in a hurry, this is an ideal fish for slapping on the barbecue.

Celery *purée*
10½ OZ/300 G CELERY HEARTS/ROOTS
6½ TBSP/3½ FL OZ/100 ML MILK
6½ TBSP/3½ FL OZ/100 ML CREAM
6½ TBSP/3½ FL OZ/100 ML WATER

Onion *purée*
7 OZ/200 G ONION
7 FL OZ/210 ML DRY RED WINE
3½ TBSP/1¾ FL OZ/50 ML CRÈME DE CASSIS/
BLACKCURRANT LIQUEUR

Broccoli *purée*
10 OZ/300 G BROCCOLI
3½ TBSP/1¾ FL OZ/50 ML OLIVE OIL

Seasoning
SALT
SEA SALT
TEN FLAVORED PEPPER

Biscuit
1½ TBSP/½ FL OZ/15 ML OLIVE *TAPENADE*
1 EGG WHITE
1½ OZ/45 G BUTTER

Fish
8 RED MULLET
3½ TBSP/1¾ FL OZ/50 ML OLIVE OIL
1 GARLIC CLOVE

Preparation time: 1 hour
Cooking time: 45 minutes
Serves 4 people

For the celery *purée*, peel and cut the celery into cubes. Cook the celery covered in equal quantities of milk and water for 20 minutes. Drain, then blend or process with the cream into a *purée*.

For the onion *purée,* peel and slice the onions. Place in a pan and simmer in the red wine and cassis. Once the onions are cooked, blend or process to a *purée*. Season to taste.

For the broccoli *purée* cut the broccoli into medium-sized florets. Cook in boiling salted water. Once cooked, run under cold water, drain and blend with the olive oil to *purée*. Season to taste.

Mix together the biscuit ingredients until smooth. Spread the batter on a non-stick baking sheet, making small rounds with your finger. Bake in a preheated oven at 350°F/180°C for 4 minutes.

Scale, clean and cut the fish into fillets. Wash and pat the fillets dry. Once ready to serve, cook skin side for 15 seconds in hot olive oil and garlic.

Arrange the fillets in a star shape in the center of a plate. Next, place a scoop of each *purée* between the fillets, with a biscuit on top of each *purée*.

Ragoût de poissons du marché sur des pommes de terre safranées

RAGOÛT OF MARKET FISH ON BUTTERED SAFFRON POTATOES

Ragoût is a stew made from meat, poultry, game, fish, or vegetables. The French word *ragoût* dates from 1642; in classic French, it was used to describe anything that stimulated the appetite or, in a figurative sense, awoke interest. For a fish *ragoût*, you must choose a fish that has a flesh firm enough to withstand the cooking, such as turbot, John Dory, red mullet, red snapper or sea bass. The method used to prepare the potatoes for this dish is the same as that used to prepare duck *confit*.

Ragoût
1 LB 2 OZ/510 G FRESH WHITE FISH FILLETS
1 GARLIC CLOVE
1¾ OZ/50 G SHALLOTS
¾ OZ/20 G CHOPPED PARSLEY
6½ TBSP/3½ FL OZ/105 ML FISH STOCK
3½ TBSP/1¾ FL OZ/50 ML DRY WHITE WINE
3½ TBSP/1¾ FL OZ/50 ML *CRÈME FRAÎCHE*/SOUR CREAM
¼ TSP/2 G SAFFRON

Potatoes
2 LARGE POTATOES
7 OZ/200 G CLARIFIED BUTTER
¼ TSP/2 G SAFFRON
SALT
PEPPER

Green vegetables
3½ OZ/100 G PEAS
3½ OZ/100 G SWEET PEAS
3½ OZ/100 G STRING BEANS

Preparation time: 1 hour
Cooking time: 30 minutes
Serves 4 people

Clean and cut the fresh fish fillets into cubes. In a pot, bring the crushed garlic, diced shallots, parsley, fish stock, and white wine to a boil. A few minutes before serving, poach the fish in the liquid. When the fish is cooked, take it out and set aside; continue to heat, the pot, reducing the liquid by one third. Remove from the heat, and add the *crème fraîche* and saffron. Check the seasoning, adding salt and pepper to taste. This is now the sauce or broth. Cut each potato into a cube shape. To do this, take the potato and cut off each end as well as each side, so that you are left with a cube. Then using a serrated knife, or a *mandoline* with a serrated edge, slice each cube, keeping all the slices together to again form the cube, and cook them in clarified butter seasoned with salt and saffron. To cook through, you can spread the cubes out like a pack of cards.

For the green vegetables, cook the peas, sweet peas and string beans in boiling salted water. Run under cold water. When ready to serve, reheat in a little water and olive oil.

Place the potatoes in the center of a soup bowl with the fish on top. Arrange the green vegetables around the bowl. Pour on the hot broth.

Étouffée de rouget gratinée et son embeurrée de choux

GRATIN OF RED SNAPPER AND BRAISED CABBAGE

Deconstructed, this fish pie shares some similarities with traditional English cooking. The snapper is stewed with vegetables and wine. It's put into a gratin dish on a bed of braised cabbage, covered with a puff pastry lid and baked. And yet the preparation of the snapper (stewed in red wine) and the cabbage (cooked with *lardons* and onions) are incontrovertibly French.

Red snapper
14 oz–1 lb 2 oz/400–500 g red snapper

Red wine sauce
1¼ oz/35 g carrots
1¼ oz/35 g leeks
2 garlic cloves
1 *bouquet garni*
10 fl oz/295 ml dry red wine
3½ tbsp/1¾ fl oz/50 ml olive oil

Cabbage
7 oz/200 g green cabbage
3½ oz/100 g pearl onions
1¾ oz/50 g bacon
3½ tbsp/1¾ fl oz/50 ml dry white wine
1¾ oz/50 g butter

Pastry
10½ oz/300 g puff pastry
2 tbsp chopped parsley
2 egg yolks, beaten
1¾ oz/50 g flour

Seasoning
Sea salt
Black pepper
Paprika

Preparation time: 40 minutes
Cooking time: 10 minutes
Serves 4 people

Clean and fillet the fish. Slice the fish into strips. Soak the bones of the fish in cold water and drain.

For the red wine sauce, peel and chop the vegetables. Sweat the fish bones and vegetables together in olive oil. Cover with red wine and add the *bouquet garni*. Bring to a boil, skimming occasionally, and leave to simmer for 15 minutes. Pour the liquid through a fine sieve, return to the heat and reduce by half.

Blanch the cabbage leaves for a few minutes in boiling salted water, drain, leave to cool and then shred. Peel the onions and cut in half. In a pan over a low heat, *sauté* the onions in butter; add the cabbage, bacon, salt and pepper. *Déglacer* the pan with white wine and reduce. Cover and leave simmer for 25 minutes.

Roll out the puff pastry and rub with the parsley and a little flour. Cut out circles of about ½ in./1.5 cm larger than your gratin dish. Individual gratins may be used.

In a gratin dish, place the cabbage mixture with the fish on top and season with paprika, sea salt and pepper. Pour the red wine sauce over the fish and sprinkle with parsley. Baste the rim of the gratin dish with the beaten egg yolks and seal the dish with the puff pastry. Bake in a preheated oven at 390°F/200°C for 10–15 minutes before serving.

Les viandes, la volaille et le gibier

MEATS, POULTRY AND GAME

The vocabulary of meat cookery is uniquely evocative: *daube, fricassé, blanquette, civet, pot au feu, salmis, estouffade*. It testifies to an inexorable development of *savoir-faire*, of learning how to transform raw flesh into dishes that attain the height of human ingenuity.

In France, the partnership between the farm and the kitchen has been a long-standing marriage. "Chicken from *Bresse*", "*Sisteron* lamb", "*Limousin* veal" show how influential husbandry is. All have their own *appellation contrôlée* like wine, and they are far from being the only examples.

Paradoxically, meat cookery is at its most refined when it's at opposing ends of the cooking spectrum. On the one hand, juicy underdone meat (or raw in the case of steak tartare), whether it be for a rapidly seared duck breast or a *gigot* (leg of lamb spiked with garlic) or a slice of *foie gras* is a national passion. On the other, arguably the greatest glories of French cuisine are dishes simmered long and slow like a *boeuf à la mode* or a *civet de lièvre à la royale* or a *confit de canard*.

Fricassée de poulet à l'estragon

FRICASSÉE TARRAGON CHICKEN

A *fricassée* is a well-known French dish consisting of chicken prepared in a white wine sauce (veal and lamb are also prepared this way). Formerly in France, the term denoted various kinds of *ragoût* of chicken, meat, fish or vegetables in white or brown stock. It is often suggested when preparing a *fricassée* to use 2 small chickens so that more of the best pieces of meat are available. The use of free-range chickens in this dish increases the flavor.

Chicken
3 LB 5 OZ/1½ KG FREE-RANGE CHICKEN
3½ TBSP/1¾ FL OZ/50 ML OLIVE OIL
1¾ OZ/50 G BUTTER

Aromatic accompaniments
2 GARLIC CLOVES
2½ OZ/70 G ONIONS
1 CARROT
1 STICK OF CELERY
4 BUTTON MUSHROOMS
2½ OZ/70 G LEEK WHITES
1 *BOUQUET GARNI*

Garnish
7 OZ/200 G SPLIT ORANGE LENTILS
1¾ OZ/50 G ONIONS
3½ OZ/100 G BACON
1 GARLIC CLOVE
1¾ OZ/50 G BUTTER
1 *BOUQUET GARNI*
13 TBSP/6½ FL OZ/195 ML CHICKEN STOCK
½ PT/10 FL OZ/300 ML MILK
10½ OZ/300 G CELERY HEART
1¾ OZ/50 G SHALLOTS
1 STEM FRESH TARRAGON
1¾ OZ/50 G BUTTER

Sauce
3½ TBSP/1¾ FL OZ/50 ML TARRAGON VINEGAR
6½ TBSP/3½ FL OZ/105 ML DRY WHITE WINE
1 PT/20 FL OZ/600 ML CHICKEN STOCK
6 STEMS OF FRESH TARRAGON
6½ TBSP/3½ FL OZ/105 ML HEAVY CREAM

Seasoning
BLACK PEPPER
SEA SALT

Preparation time: 1 hour
Cooking time: 45 minutes
Serves 4 people

Thoroughly rinse the chicken pieces. Peel and finely chop the aromatic accompaniments. Season the chicken and bake in the oven with a tiny amount of olive oil until browned. Remove the pan from the oven, and place it on the stove. *Déglacer* with white wine and tarragon vinegar, and reduce until the liquid has disappeared. Place the aromatic accompaniments in beside the chicken and cook on the stovetop for another 5 minutes. Cover the chicken pieces with the chicken stock and cook over the stove top, checking to remove the impurities from time to time. Take the chicken pieces out when cooked and set aside. Continue cooking the juice until it reduces by half. Pass the remaining liquid through a sieve. Add the cream and gently cook for 5 minutes. Check the seasoning.

For the garnish, cook the chopped onion, bacon and crushed garlic in butter. Add the lentils and cook for a couple of minutes longer (ensuring that the color does not change). Add the chicken stock and *bouquet garni*, seasoning and bring to a boil. Boil for 5 minutes, then reduce the heat and simmer for 30–40 minutes until the lentils are fully cooked.

Peel the celery heart with a knife and cut this into large cubes. Cook in a mixture of one part water and one part milk, with a pinch of sea salt. Cover and cook gently for 40 minutes. Drain and put the celery heart into a colander, and remove as much of the liquid as possible. Blend until it has a smooth texture. Season to taste.

Blend all the sauce ingredients until a smooth sauce consistency is achieved.

Reheat the chicken in its juice and put in the center of the plate. Put small helpings of celery *purée* and lentils around it and pour the sauce on top. Sprinkle with fresh tarragon.

Chef's tip
It is always best to use chicken pieces for this dish as the bones of the chicken help to preserve the flavors during cooking and therefore add more flavor to the finished sauce.

Mignon de porc sauté aux agrumes

PORK FILLET WITH CITRUS FRUITS

Until the 1970s, few chefs in luxury restaurants dared to put pork on the menu. Then Roger Vergé of the *Moulin de Mougins* near Cannes (who had worked in the Caribbean) introduced it, serving it with citrus fruit to cut the richness of the meat. Since then it has never gone out of favor, even though it belongs to the *Nouvelle Cuisine* era.

Pork
1 LB 5 OZ/595 G PORK FILLET
3½ TBSP/1¾ FL OZ/50 ML OLIVE OIL
3½ OZ/100 G SUGAR
13 TBSP/6¾ FL OZ/195 ML PORK OR CHICKEN STOCK

Citrus fruit
1 ORANGE
1 PINK GRAPEFRUIT
1 LEMON

Garnish
12 BABY CARROTS
1 OZ/30 G BUTTER
1¼ OZ/40 G HONEY
7 OZ/200 G GOLDEN APPLES
7 OZ/200 G PEARS
7 OZ/200 G PEARL ONIONS
3½ TBSP/1¾ FL OZ/50 ML BALSAMIC VINEGAR
1 TSP/5 G POWDERED GINGER
1 TSP/5 G SUGAR
1 BRANCH FRESH TARRAGON
4 SAGE LEAVES

Seasoning
SALT
GROUND PEPPER

Preparation time: 30 minutes
Cooking time: 20 minutes
Serves 4 people

Cut the pork fillet into medallions, creating three per person. Sear in olive oil and then remove from the pan. In the pan, add the sugar and caramelize. *Déglacer* with the juice of the citrus fruits and reduce. Add the pork and cook through; check the seasoning.

For the garnish, peel the carrots and blanch for 3–4 minutes. *Sauté* the carrots in butter and glaze with a little honey. Peel and cut the apples and pears into cubes. *Sauté* in butter and sugar until the mixture has the consistency of chutney. Peel the pearl onions, cook in butter and sugar, then *déglacer* with vinegar. Season with powdered ginger.

Place the medallions in a star shape around the plate, with the onions in the center. Place a spoon of the carrot on the plate along with the fruit chutney. Decorate with the sage and fresh tarragon.

La casserole d'agneau et sa printanière

LAMB CASSEROLE WITH SPRING VEGETABLES

With the addition of white wine (or even a light red) this lamb stew becomes a well-known *cuisine bourgeoise* dish *navarin printanière*. Change the lamb for beef and marinate it in wine before cooking: *daube de boeuf*. Switch it for veal; add herbs and its *sauté de veau provençale*. The family of casserole dishes is closely interrelated. Once you master one, you can tackle them all with confidence.

Lamb
1¾ LB/800 G BONED LAMB SHOULDER
3½ TBSP/1¾ FL OZ/50 ML OLIVE OIL
1 OZ/30 G FLOUR
1 OZ/30 G TOMATO CONCENTRATE
2¾ OZ/80 G ONION
2 GARLIC CLOVES
1 *BOUQUET GARNI*

Vegetables
13½ OZ/385 G POTATOES
4¼ OZ/130 G PEARL ONIONS
8½ OZ/240 G CARROT
1 GARLIC CLOVE
9 OZ/255 G TURNIPS
1¾ OZ/50 G PEAS
1¾ OZ/50 G GREEN BEANS
3½ TBSP/1¾ FL OZ/50 ML OLIVE OIL

Seasoning
SEA SALT
SALT
GROUND PEPPER
SUGAR
¾ OZ/20 G CHOPPED PARSLEY

Preparation time: 1 hour
Cooking time: 55 minutes
Serves 4 people

Cut the lamb into cubes; place the lamb in a pan and season with salt and pepper. *Sauté* the lamb in olive oil. Peel and mince the garlic and onion. Add these and the tomato concentrate to the pan. Sweat for a few minutes. Sprinkle with flour and bake at 390°F/200°C for 5 minutes. Add enough water to the pan to cover the lamb, add the *bouquet garni*, salt and pepper and bring to a boil over a burner. Remove from the stove; place in the covered pan and continue to cook in a preheated oven at 355°/180°C for 40–50 minutes.

To prepare the potatoes, carrots and the turnips, peel and cut the vegetables into cylindrical shapes. Brown the potatoes in butter, olive oil, garlic and thyme until cooked. Cook the carrots and turnips separately in water, sugar, butter, salt and pepper. When tender, strain the carrots and lightly brown in a pan with a little butter.

Cook the peas and green beans in boiling, salted water, and then run under cold water. Reheat in a couple of tablespoons of the cooking liquid surrounding the lamb.

Place the meat in the center of the plate and place the different vegetables around the meat. Cover with the casserole liquid and decorate with chopped parsley.

Chef's tip
A light red wine can replace the water that is used in this recipe.

Civet de lièvre

HARE STEW

The word *civet* derives from an old French word for onions, but until recently the word was associated with a technique of thickening the sauce of this rustic hare stew with the animal's blood. Nowadays, though, it's more common to use a *roux* of flour and butter. Rabbit can be used if it proves difficult to find hare.

Hare
6 LB/3 KG HARE
3½ TBSP/1¾ FL OZ/50 ML OLIVE OIL

Marinade
1 CARROT
1 ONION
3 GARLIC CLOVES
½ STICK OF CELERY
½ LEEK (GREEN PORTION ONLY)
1 *BOUQUET GARNI*
13 TBSP/6½ FL OZ/200 ML OLIVE OIL
6½ TBSP/3¼ FL OZ/100 ML DRY RED WINE VINEGAR
1¾ PT/1 LITER DRY RED WINE
3 JUNIPER BERRIES
1 CLOVE
5 PEPPERCORNS

Roux
1 OZ/30 G BUTTER
1 OZ/30 G FLOUR

Vegetable garnish
12 PEARL ONIONS
12 SMALL MUSHROOMS
1¼ OZ/40 G BACON
8 TRIANGULAR SHAPED SLICES OF WHOLEMEAL BREAD
1¾ OZ/50 G BUTTER
1¾ OZ/50 G CHOPPED PARSLEY
1¾ OZ/50 G SUGAR

Fresh pasta
SEE FRESH PASTA RECIPE IN THE ITALIAN FIRST COURSES SECTION (P. 169).

Preparation time: 2 hours (marinating the hare 48 hours)
Cooking time: 1 hour 30 minutes
Serves 4 people

Cut hare at the joints and place the pieces in a large pot. To make the marinade, cut up all the vegetables into a *mirepoix* and cover the hare. Cover completely with the red wine, oil and seasonings. Leave the hare to marinade for at least 48 hours.

After the specified marinating time, remove the pieces of hare and pat dry. Heat the marinade in a saucepan and *flambé*. In a separate pan, brown the hare pieces in olive oil and season with salt and pepper. Take the hare out of the pan and set aside. Take the pan and melt the butter from the *roux* ingredients, stir in the flour; you now have a *roux*. Pour the marinating liquid into the pan with the *roux*, stir continuously until the sauce begins to thicken. Bring this to a boil to remove any acidity from the wine.

Place the hare pieces back into the pan with the sauce and continue to cook for 1½ hours on low heat. At the end of the cooking time, remove the meat and pass the liquid through a fine sieve (this is now your sauce). Replace the hare pieces and reheat before serving.

Cook the pearl onions in a pan covered with water, salt, pepper and sugar. Cover the onions with a round of wax paper and cook on a medium heat until all the liquid has evaporated and the onions are lightly browned. Add these to the hare stew.

Slice the mushrooms thinly and *sauté* with the diced bacon. Add these to the hare stew.

Brush the bread slices with melted butter, and sprinkle with chopped parsley. Bake in the oven until golden.

Place the pasta in a bowl and cover with the hare stew. Serve with the toast slices on the side.

Filet de bœuf grillé et ses petits légumes, sauce Béarnaise

GRILLED FILLET OF BEEF WITH BABY VEGETABLES
AND BÉARNAISE SAUCE

Order a steak in a restaurant and you should ask for it *Bleu* – so rare it's only tepid in the middle; *Saignant* – rare; *A point* – medium; *Bien cuit* – well-done. *Béarnaise* sauce is a classic buttery sauce, belonging to the same family as *Hollandaise*. It's the perfect partner for all grilled meat.

Beef
4 *TOURNEDOS*/BEEF TENDERLOIN FILLETS
3½ TBSP/1¾ FL OZ/50 ML OLIVE OIL

Béarnaise **sauce**
1 SHALLOT
3½ TBSP/1¾ FL OZ/50 ML TARRAGON VINEGAR
1 TSP/5 G BLACK PEPPERCORNS
1 SPRIG OF TARRAGON
2 EGG YOLKS
7 OZ/200 G CLARIFIED BUTTER
3½ TBSP/1¾ FL OZ/50 ML WATER

Garnish
4 MINI SPRING ONIONS
8 MINI ZUCCHINI
1¾ OZ/50 G GRATED PARMESAN
1 TURNIP
1 POTATO
1 SPRIG OF THYME
1 GARLIC CLOVE
1 BAY LEAF
6½ TBSP/3½ FL OZ/105 ML VEAL OR BEEF STOCK

Chef's tip

A Béarnaise sauce, which has curdled, can be saved by gradually beating in a tablespoon of hot water (if the sauce is cold) or cold water (if the sauce is hot).

Preparation time: 30 minutes
Cooking time: 30 minutes
Serves 4 people

For the *Béarnaise* sauce, mince the shallot and crushed black peppercorns in a mortar and pestle. In a pan, reduce the vinegar, shallot, pepper and tarragon until almost all the liquid has evaporated. Add the egg yolks and three spoonfuls of water, and whisk together until creamy. Take off the heat and add the clarified butter by droplets. Strain the sauce and reserve as it is in a *bain-marie*.

For the garnish, blanch the mini spring onions and mini zucchini in boiling salted water. When tender, remove and run under cold water. Just before serving, reheat the spring onions and zucchini in a little olive oil and sprinkle with Parmesan. *Tourner* the turnip and potatoes. *Sauté* in olive oil and butter with some thyme, garlic and the bay leaf. Add the veal or beef stock, cover the pan and continue to cook on a gentle heat until tender.

Oil the meat and season with salt and pepper. Grill the meat to preference.

Slice the meat and place it in the center of the plate. Place the vegetables on top. Slice the zucchini into a fan shape by running a knife down the length of the zucchini at regular intervals, leaving the top intact. Press the zucchini down so that it fans out the slices. Serve the sauce separately.

Émincé d'autriche et sa cassolette de légumes

FANNED OSTRICH AND VEGETABLE STEW

The idea of this recipe comes from a very nice Italian dish "the *tagliata*", which is made out of beef. Ostrich is a very good substitute, but you can also use chicken or duck breast.

Ostrich
13½ OZ/400 G OSTRICH FILLET
6¾ OZ/200 G *FOIE GRAS* (FRESH)
4 BUTTON MUSHROOMS
1 BUNCH CHERVIL

Stew
4 JERUSALEM ARTICHOKES
4 TURNIPS
8 FINGERLING POTATOES
3½ TBSP/1¾ FL OZ/50 ML OLIVE OIL
1¾ OZ/50 G BUTTER
1 *BOUQUET GARNI*
3½ TBSP/1¾ FL OZ/50 ML DRY RED WINE
8½ FL OZ/300 ML CHICKEN STOCK
¾ OZ/20 G CHOPPED PARSLEY

Seasoning
COARSE SALT
FINE SALT
BLACK PEPPERCORNS

Preparation time: 30 minutes
Cooking time: 50 minutes
Serves 4 people

Finely slice the ostrich fillet, *foie gras*, and mushrooms.
Place three layers of ostrich, *foie gras* and mushrooms each 4 in./10 cm in thickness. Add salt and pepper and cook for 1 minute in the oven at 480°F/250°C just before serving.

For the stew, peel and cut the Jerusalem artichokes, turnips and potatoes into slices and blanch in salted water. Drain and *sauté* in olive oil and butter until they start to brown. Add salt and pepper. *Déglacer* in red wine and reduce. Add the chicken stock and *bouquet garni* and bring to a boil. Cook in the oven at 355°F/180°C to caramelize the vegetables.

Serve in a fan shape on a plate with sprigs of chervil. Serve the vegetables in a separate casserole dish.

Le carré d'agneau au safran, échalotes confites

RACK OF LAMB WITH SAFFRON AND SHALLOTS

Lamb is the predominant meat served in Provence and is a popular dish throughout France. A lamb often appears in the "coat of arms" of butchers' guilds, particularly in Paris. Lamb is preferred young, and is most often served rare. Here the lamb is prepared with saffron and shallots for additional flavor.

Lamb
3 LB 5 OZ/1½ KG RACK OF LAMB
SALT AND PEPPER TO SEASON
13 TBSP/6½ FL OZ/195 ML OF OLIVE OIL
1 CLOVE OF GARLIC

Sauce
16½ FL OZ/490 ML LAMB STOCK (OR CHICKEN STOCK)
½ TSP/2 G SAFFRON

Shallots
12 SHALLOTS
13 TBSP/6½ FL OZ/195 ML SUNFLOWER OIL
2 TBSP *HERBS DE PROVENCE*

Vegetables
7 OZ/200 G BROCCOLI

Preparation time: 1 hour 20 minutes
Cooking time: 30 minutes
Serves 4 people

Prepare the shallots first. Cut off the root end of the shallot, but leave the skin on. Cook the shallots slowly over low heat for 1 hour in oil seasoned with *herbs de Provence*.

Season the lamb with salt and pepper. Sear the meat in olive oil, skin-side down, on a roasting tray. Turn the piece of meat over, sprinkle with the saffron and roast in a preheated oven for approximately 25 minutes at 355°F/180°C. Once cooked, leave the meat on a rack for several minutes before slicing. Cut the rack of lamb into two chops per portion.

To prepare the sauce, *déglacer* the roasting pan with lamb stock, reduce and strain. Blend or process the liquid until a good consistency has been achieved. Add the saffron just before serving.

Cook the broccoli in boiling salted water. Once tender, strain the broccoli and run it under cold water. Before serving, reheat the broccoli in a pan with some of the lamb stock.

Place the vegetables in the center of the plate. Take the lamb chops and cross them on the vegetables and carefully pour some of the sauce over the lamb and around the plate.

Chef's tip
Suckling lamb is recommended for this recipe, as the meat is very tender.

Les fonds

STOCKS

Stocks are often referred to as the "foundations of cuisine", due to the fact that they are the bases for many recipes. White and brown stocks, which used to be essential bases for almost all the great classic sauces, take a long time to make and are often expensive to prepare and hence are not often used in modern cuisine. The advent of stock cubes or commercial stocks that can be purchased in stores has reduced the use of traditional stocks. A well-made stock, however, can greatly enhance the final flavor of a dish. The following are several stocks used in various recipes throughout this book.

Veau fond

VEAL STOCK

Makes 1¾ PT/1 LITER of stock

2¼ LB/1 KG VEAL BONES AND TRIMMINGS
1 LARGE CARROT
1 LARGE YELLOW ONION
1 CELERY STICK
1 LB 2 OZ/500 G OZ FRESH TOMATOES
3½ PT/2 LITERS WATER
1¾ OZ/50 G MUSHROOM PEELINGS
½ OZ/15 G TOMATO CONCENTRATE
2 GARLIC CLOVES
1 STEM OF THYME
½ BAY LEAF
1 STEM OF PARSLEY
PEPPER

In an oven preheated to 430°F/220°C, brown the bones and trimmings on a baking tray together with the unpeeled onion, cut in half. Add the rest of the vegetables and roast for 4–5 minutes, turning occasionally. Take the tray out of the oven and transfer its contents into a saucepan, leaving any fat. Add the concentrated tomatoes and herbs and cover with cold water. Bring the stock to a boil and simmer over a gentle heat for 1 hour, occasionally skimming off any impurities that rise to the surface. Pass through a sieve and store in the refrigerator when cool.

Poulet fond

CHICKEN STOCK

Makes 1¾ PT/1 LITER of stock

2¼ LB/1 KG CHICKEN BONES
1 CARROT
1 SMALL CELERY STICK
1 YELLOW ONION
1 WHITE OF SMALL LEEK
2 GARLIC CLOVES
1 STEM THYME
½ BAY LEAF
1 STEM PARSLEY
SALT
BLACK PEPPER
3½ PT/2 LITERS WATER

Put the chicken carcasses in a heavy-bottomed pot with the finely chopped vegetables, herbs and seasoning. Cover with water, bring to a boil and simmer on a gentle heat for 2 hours. Occasionally skim off any impurities that rise to the surface. Pass through a sieve and store in the refrigerator when cool.

Les fromages

CHEESE DISHES

"To make a nice change from the traditional cheese platter, I give you a few hot and cold cheese suggestions, which you can make. These quick and easy recipes can be used as an appetizer or between the main course and the dessert, or they could be offered as a good snack during the day. Besides being delicious, if you prepare them and do not eat them right away, they make wonderful leftovers."

Frédéric Rivière

La terrine au Roquefort

ROQUEFORT TERRINE

The veined Roquefort cheese, made from goat's milk and ripened in caves, is as well known in France as Stilton is in England. Because of its strong flavor, it lends itself to marriages with nuts and fruit. When eaten by itself, it's often mixed with a little softened butter.

Terrine
3½ OZ/100 G GOLDEN DELICIOUS APPLES
7 OZ/200 G ROQUEFORT
2¼ OZ/60 G WALNUTS
2¼ OZ/60 G RAISINS
2¼ OZ/60 G HEAVY CREAM
7 OZ/200 G FRESH FIGS

Vinaigrette
4 TBSP/2 FL OZ/60 ML WALNUT OIL
2 TBSP/1 FL OZ/30 ML SUNFLOWER OIL
2 TBSP/1 FL OZ/30 ML CIDER VINEGAR
FINE SALT TO TASTE
GROUND PEPPER TO TASTE

Salad
1 OZ/30 G CHOPPED CHIVES
3½ OZ/100 G LOLA ROSSA/RED LEAF LETTUCE

Preparation time: 3 hours
Cooking time: 6 hours for the apples
Serves 4 people

To prepare the terrine, peel and slice the apples into fine slivers. Dry them out in the oven at 250°F/120°C for about 6 hours. Mix together the Roquefort, nuts, raisins and cream. Using four small, bottomless ring molds; line the sides with sliced figs. Fill the mold with the cheese mixture and pack down firmly. Let this set in the refrigerator for at least 1 hour.

Dissolve the salt and pepper into the vinegar. Whisk in the oils and set aside.

Place the lettuce leaves in the center of a serving plate. Remove the terrine from the mold and place on the lettuce. Insert slivers of dried apple into the terrine, sprinkle drops of vinaigrette around the terrine and plate, and decorate with chopped chives.

Chef's tip
As you start your day, you can put the apple in the oven, and you will have an excellent terrine for supper.

Tartelettes de fromage soufflé

CHEESE SOUFFLÉ TARTLETS

The most famous mountain cheeses are Emmental, Beaufort, Comté, Cantal and Swiss Gruyère, which all make excellent *soufflés*. They are all large cheeses, but unlike Parmesan, pieces will dry out quickly even when carefully handled. Buy in small quantities and use as soon as possible. Packets of pre-grated cheese are often made from inferior quality cheese.

Tartlets
7 OZ/200 G PUFF PASTRY
¾ OZ/20 G FLOUR
UNCOOKED RICE OR CHICKPEAS

Cheese *soufflé*
5 EGGS
10½ OZ/300 G BUTTER
8¾ OZ/250 G GRATED GRUYÈRE
GROUND BLACK PEPPER

Vinaigrette
4 TBSP/2 FL OZ/60 ML HAZELNUT OIL
2 TBSP/1 FL OZ/30 ML SUNFLOWER OIL
2 TBSP/1 FL OZ/30 ML AGED BALSAMIC VINEGAR
FINE SALT
GROUND BLACK PEPPER
1 CHERVIL SPRIG, CHOPPED
1 TBSP CHIVES, CHOPPED

Salad
7 OZ/200 G RED LETTUCE LEAVES

Preparation time: 20 minutes
Cooking time: 9 minutes
Serves 4 people

Roll out the pastry dough to approximately ¼ in./7 mm. With a cookie cutter, cut out 12 circles approximately 2½ in./6 cm in diameter. Place the circles in individual tart molds. Prick the dough with a fork, cover with uncooked rice or chickpeas to keep the center from rising. Pre-bake at 390°F/200°C for 4 minutes. Once cooked, remove the chickpeas or rice.

For the cheese *soufflé*, in a bowl, mix together all the ingredients and season with freshly ground black pepper. Fill the tart shells with the *soufflé* mix and continue to cook for another 5 minutes at 390°F/200°C.

Dissolve the salt and pepper in the vinegar. Whisk in the oils and add the herbs.

In a bowl, toss the salad in the vinaigrette. Place some salad in the center of a plate and place the tartlets around the salad.

Brochettes de fromages aux fruits

CHEESE AND FRUIT KEBABS

This refreshing dish is perfect for *al fresco* dining.

Brochette
3½ oz/100 g apple
3½ oz/100 g pear
Juice of 1 lemon
3½ oz/100 g fig
3½ oz/100 g Beaufort cheese (Emmental or Gruyère as substitutes)
3½ oz/100 g goats' cheese
3½ oz/100 g Parmesan cheese
Bamboo or wooden skewers, skewer size is dependent on plate size

Vinaigrette
1 tbsp Dijon mustard
2 tbsp/1 fl oz/30 ml balsamic vinegar
4 tbsp/2 fl oz/60 ml olive oil
2 tbsp/1 fl oz/30 ml sunflower oil
2 tbsp/1 fl oz/30 ml water
Fine salt
Ground pepper

Salad
7 oz/200 g lamb's-ear lettuce/mache or cos/romaine lettuce

Preparation time: 10 minutes
Cooking time: 5 minutes
Serves 4 people

To prepare the *brochettes*, peel, core and seed the apple and the pear. Cut the fruit into cubes (¾ in./2 cm square) and sprinkle with lemon juice. Next, cut the fig into quarters and the cheeses into cubes and alternate the different ingredients along the wooden skewers.

For the vinaigrette, mix together the mustard, vinegar, salt and pepper. Little by little, incorporate the oils. Add approximately 2 tablespoons of water to help separate the oils.

In a bowl, toss the salad in the vinaigrette. Cover a plate with the salad. Warm the *brochettes* in the oven for a few minutes so the cheese melts very slightly and place these on top of the salad.

Salade de chèvre chaud

WARM GOAT CHEESE SALAD

Various kinds of goat cheese are suitable for this popular dish. Individual discs of medium ripe cheese are best, because they start to melt when grilled but hold their shape. The toasted pine nuts are a delicate personal touch of Frédéric Rivière's.

Goat cheese
4 FIRM SMALL ROUND GOAT CHEESES
8 SLICES OF COUNTRY BREAD OR MULTI GRAIN BREAD
1 OZ/30 G PINE NUTS
GROUND BLACK PEPPER
3½ TBSP/1¾ FL OZ/50 ML OLIVE OIL

Vinaigrette
4 TBSP/2 FL OZ/60 ML SESAME SEED OIL
2 TBSP/1 FL OZ/30 ML SUNFLOWER OIL
2 TBSP/1 FL OZ/30 ML SHERRY VINEGAR
FINE SALT TO TASTE
GROUND PEPPER TO TASTE

Caramel liquid
3½ OZ/100 G SUGAR
4 TBSP/2 FL OZ/60 ML WATER

Salad
7 OZ/200 G MIXED SALAD LEAVES
2 SPRIGS OF CHERVIL

Preparation time: 15 minutes
Cooking time: 2 minutes
Serves 4 people

Cut the cheese in half lengthwise and place little halves on a square or round of the bread. Sprinkle with pine nuts, ground pepper and oil. Place under the grill for about 30 seconds.

Dissolve the salt and pepper in the vinegar. Whisk in the oils and set aside.

Dissolve the sugar in a little water over medium heat. When light caramel syrup is obtained, add the remaining water. Bring to a boil and cook for 1 minute. Set aside.

In a bowl, toss the salad in the vinaigrette. Make two small "nests" of salad on a plate and place the goats' cheese breads on top. Pour a thin stream of the caramel liquid across the salad leaves. Decorate the entire dish with sprigs of chervil.

Petits soufflés au Parmesan

INDIVIDUAL PARMESAN SOUFFLÉS

Nothing more than the classic cheese *soufflé* recipe but baked in single portion *ramekins*. The accompanying salad and sauce make a refreshing contrast.

Soufflé base
1 OZ/30 G BUTTER
1 OZ/30 G FLOUR
8½ FL OZ/250 ML MILK
2½ OZ/70 G PARMESAN
3 EGG WHITES, SEPARATED
1 OZ/30 G PARMESAN FOR DECORATION

Sauce
2 TOMATOES
¾ OZ/20 G BLACK OLIVES
3½ TBSP/1¾ FL OZ/50 ML BALSAMIC VINEGAR
FINE SALT
GROUND PEPPER

Salad
2 HEADS OF ENDIVE
½ OZ/15 G WALNUTS
½ OZ/15 G HAZELNUTS
½ OZ/15 G PINE NUTS
½ OZ/15 G CHERVIL
½ OZ/15 G BASIL

Preparation time: 25 minutes
Cooking time: 9 minutes
Serves 4 people

For the *soufflé*, melt the butter over medium heat and incorporate the flour. Add the milk, bring to a boil, and cook for 2–3 minutes. Take the pan from the heat and stir in the egg yolks, return to the heat, and cook for another 2 minutes. Add 2½ oz/70 g of Parmesan. Beat the egg whites until stiff and gently fold into this mixture. Pour into individual buttered-and-floured *soufflé* molds or *ramekins* approximately 1½–2½ in./4–6 cm in diameter. Sprinkle the remaining 1 oz/30 g of Parmesan on top. Bake in a preheated oven at 425°F/220°C for 2 minutes, then reduce the temperature to 390°F/200°C and cook for another 7 minutes. Serve immediately.

Peel, seed and chop the tomatoes into cubes. Pit and slice the olives into rounds. Mix together the tomato, vinegar, olives and season.

Finely slice the endive. Mix together with the nuts and herbs. Season with salt and pepper.

Serve the *soufflé* on a plate and the salad in a bowl on the side.

Les pains

BREADS

The whole world loves French bread. The long, golden baguette and its big sister the *pain parisien* are relative newcomers, only becoming popular in the twentieth century. Recently, both have been under fire as factories supplying supermarkets have sought to supplant craft bakers. Fortunately the *boulangers artisanaux* have fought back, pointing out the shortcomings of the mass-produced loaves and highlighting the qualities of their own hand-made products. Their stand has stimulated interest in traditional baking. Slow-fermented sourdough *pains de campagne*, baked in wood-fired ovens, fetch a premium. Regional breads such as the Provençal *fougasse* or olive breads have never been so popular. Some chefs even prefer baking their own loaves.

Any bread, good or indifferent, smells appetizing when it comes out of the oven. It's only after it has cooled that one can judge its quality. The crisp crust on a baguette is a sign of freshness. It should never be leathery. Its crumb will show how it's been made. It should have an open, chewy texture with irregular air pockets. Country and rye loaves won't go stale for several days and if they've been fermented with a *levain*, have a more pronounced flavor.

Le pain de mie

SANDWICH BREAD

1 LB/450 G WHEAT FLOUR
½ TSP SALT
½ OZ/15 G FRESH YEAST OR 2 TBSP DRY YEAST
10 FL OZ/295 ML WARM MILK
½ TSP MALT EXTRACT
1 OZ/30 G BUTTER

Preparation time: 1 hour 45 minutes
Cooking time: 35 minutes
Serves 4 people

Sift together the flour and salt. Dissolve the yeast in the warm milk and malt. Make a well in the center and add the yeast, milk and malt. Combine together and knead for 10 minutes. Cover with plastic wrap and leave to rise for 1½ hours at room temperature. Punch down the dough and leave to rise for another hour. Work the dough into a round loaf and set aside for 5 minutes. Oil a 13 × 4 × 3½ in. (33 × 10 × 9 cm) bread pan. Flatten out the dough with the palm of your hand, then form into a cylindrical shape that will fit in your bread pan – fill only by a third. Cover with plastic wrap and leave the dough to rise until three-quarters of the way up the bread pan.

Cover the pan either with a lid or wax paper weighted down. Bake at 430°F/220°C for 20 minutes. Uncover and bake for another 15 minutes. To check if ready, the bread should sound hollow when tapped.

La fougasse

FOUGASSE

This is the pretty, oval-shaped bread found all over Provence. It can be flavored with *anise*, herbs, olives, anchovies, walnuts or crisp fried *lardons* or bacon. An egg-enriched version is eaten at Christmas.

Day one
¼ OZ/7 G DRIED YEAST
5 TBSP/2½ FL OZ/75 ML WARM WATER
½ TSP SALT
1 TBSP/½ FL OZ/15 ML DRY WHITE WINE
½ TSP OLIVE OIL
5¼ OZ/150 G WHITE FLOUR

Day two
¼ OZ/7 G FRESH YEAST OR 1 TBSP DRY YEAST
11¾ FL OZ/350 ML WATER
1½ OZ/45 G WHITE FLOUR FOR DUSTING
1 TSP SALT

Glaze
1 EGG
2 TBSP/1 FL OZ/30 ML MILK

Preparation time: 2 hours 30 minutes
(prepare the dough 1 day ahead)
Cooking time: 20 minutes
Serves 4 people

Day one
Prepare the dough the day before.
Dissolve the dried yeast in warm water, wine and olive oil. Incorporate the sifted flour and salt. Cover with plastic wrap and keep refrigerated overnight.

Day two
Add the fresh, crumbled yeast, water, salt and remaining 1½ oz/45 g of flour to the dough. Knead the dough for 6 minutes. Leave the dough to stand for 1½ hours in a warm place (79°F/26°C) until doubled in volume. Divide the dough in half. Flatten out in a rectangle with the palm of your hand. Fold the ends in toward the center. Cover and leave to stand for 10 minutes.

With a rolling pin, roll out the dough into 10 × 6 in./25 × 15 cm rectangles 4 in./10 cm thick. If the dough is too sticky, leave it to stand for several minutes longer. Score the center of each rectangle with a knife. Place the rectangles on an oiled baking sheet. Cover and leave at room temperature to rise for 40 minutes.

For the glaze, whisk, in a small bowl, the egg and milk together. With a pastry brush, brush the loaves with the glaze mixture.

Bake in a preheated oven at 445°F/230°C for 20 minutes. The *fougasse* are done when they sound hollow when tapped. Leave to cool on a rack.

Les desserts

DESSERTS

Dessert is the last impression a diner takes away from a meal, so it's impossible to overstate its importance. Because it's not eaten on an empty stomach, it has to be uniquely tempting, even if it's only a perfectly ripe, fragrant peach. In France, many families will buy a *gâteau* or a *tarte* from the local *pâtisserie*, but a simple (or not too difficult!) dessert made freshly at home can match their most exotic concoctions. Ice creams and sorbets, freshly made, will always taste better than store-bought ones. A home cook's chocolate sauce can match the professional's version.

Unlike other branches of cooking, where ingredients are an *aide mémoire* (but open to some modification) once a cook becomes experienced, *pâtisserie* requires careful weighing and also a regard for ambient conditions. That's why many chefs prefer handling doughs on marble tops, which stay cool even when the kitchen is hot.

The good thing about desserts, from the home cook's point of view is that, *soufflés* apart, they are prepared in advance. They aren't made under pressure. He or she can sit down at the table confident that the climax to the meal is going to be a hit.

Les trois crèmes brûlées du moment

THREE CRÈMES BRÛLÉES

This famous dessert, also known as burnt cream or Trinity cream, is rich custard protected by a sugary crust that is broiled golden brown. This well-known French dessert is actually claimed by the English as their own, although its lineage is often debated. Using the techniques mentioned in this recipe, try creating your own distinctive flavors.

Chocolate *crème*
1½ EGG YOLKS
1 OZ/30 G SUGAR
½ OZ/15 G UNSWEETENED CHOCOLATE POWDER
4 TBSP/2 FL OZ/60 ML MILK
10 TBSP/5 FL OZ/150 ML WHIPPING CREAM

Grand Marnier *crème*
1½ EGG YOLKS
1 OZ/30 G SUGAR
6½ TBSP/3½ FL OZ/105 ML GRAND MARNIER
6½ TBSP/3½ FL OZ/105 ML MILK
10 TBSP/5 FL OZ/150 ML WHIPPING CREAM

Raspberry *crème*
1½ EGG YOLKS
1 OZ/30 G SUGAR
13½ FL OZ/400 ML MILK
10 TBSP/5 FL OZ/150 ML WHIPPING CREAM
12 FRESH RASPBERRIES

Sugar cages
10½ OZ/300 G SUGAR
2 TBSP/1 FL OZ/30 ML WATER
½ OZ/15 G KARO/ GLUCOSE SYRUP
BROWN SUGAR FOR DECORATION

Preparation time: 30 minutes
Cooking time: 1 hour
Serves 4 people

To prepare the chocolate *crème*, in a bowl, mix together the egg yolks, sugar, and chocolate powder. Strain the milk and whipping cream into this mixture. Pour into four individual *ramekins*. Bake at 195°F/90°C for approximately 1 hour.

For the Grand Marnier *crème*, mix together in a bowl the egg yolks and sugar. Add the remaining ingredients and pour into four individual *ramekins*. Bake at 195°F/90°C for approximately 1 hour.

For the raspberry *crème*, in a bowl, mix together the egg yolks and sugar. Add milk and whipping cream. Place several raspberries in the bottom of each *ramekin* and cover with the cream mixture. Bake at 190°F/90°C for approximately 1 hour.

To test if the *brûlées* are cooked, gently move the dish. The cream should neither be floppy nor liquid, nor hard.

To make the sugar cages, in a pot over low heat, caramelize the sugar and water. Oil the bottom of a bowl (not plastic) and turn it upside down. Using a spoon, drip the caramelized sugar mixture over the upturned bowl in a pattern of your choice (like a cage or lace cap); repeat several times to make as many cages as you wish. Leave the mixture to cool, and then carefully remove the sugar cage from the bowl. You should now have a bowl shape made out of caramel.

Sprinkle the creams with a small amount of brown sugar. Brown using a blowtorch or carefully under the grill. Put the three mini *crèmes brûlées* under a sugar cage and serve.

Chef's tip
This trio uses dried/powdered, liqueur and fresh fruit based ingredients. Experiment with substitutes such as dried herbs (lavender, thyme) for the chocolate; Mandarin Imperial for the Grand Marnier; and bananas, strawberries, or blueberries for the raspberries. When using herbs, steep them in hot milk first, and strain them as in the recipe.

Les contrastes

THE CONTRASTS

Working with sugar is part of the professional pastry chef's craft, but this "artist's palette" made to display fruit, a sorbet and a *sabayon* is a simple introduction to sugar boiling techniques. You can, of course, eat the palette, but it's really just for decorative purposes.

Palettes
1¾ OZ/50 G KARO/GLUCOSE SYRUP
6½ TBSP/3½ FL OZ/105 ML WATER
1 LB 2 OZ/510 G SUGAR
FOOD COLORINGS OF YOUR CHOICE

Sabayon
2 EGG YOLKS
1¾ OZ/50 G SUGAR
3½ TBSP/1¾ FL OZ/50 ML DRY WHITE WINE OR CHAMPAGNE

Sorbet
4¼ OZ/130 G SUGAR
8½ FL OZ/250 ML WATER
ZESTE OF 1 LIME
4 TBSP/2 FL OZ/60 ML LEMON JUICE

Fruit
3½ OZ/100 G RASPBERRIES
3½ OZ/100 G STRAWBERRIES
3½ OZ/100 G BLUEBERRIES
3½ OZ/100 G RED CURRANTS OR RAISINS

Preparation time: 40 minutes plus the processing of the ice cream
Serves 4 people

Heat the Karo, sugar and water together until the mixture reaches 300°F/150°C on a candy thermometer. Be sure that the mixture does not caramelize. Spread different food colorings on wax paper squares, you can make any patterns that you wish. Pour the sugar mixture over the food colorings in any shape or pattern you wish. Leave to harden.

Mix all the *sabayon* ingredients together in a bowl. Over a low heat, whisk the mixture with a wire whisk until creamy. Set aside.

In a pan, mix together the sugar, water and lime *zeste*. Bring the mixture to a boil and continue to cook for 15 minutes. Remove the lime *zeste* and add the lemon juice. Leave the mixture to cool. Process in an ice cream machine.

Remove the colored palettes from the wax paper and place in the center of a plate. Place a scoop of sorbet in the center of a palette and the different berries around the sorbet. Cover with the *sabayon*. Brown with a blowtorch and serve immediately.

La poire au vin rouge et sa glace au lait d'amandes

PEAR IN RED WINE WITH ALMOND MILK ICE CREAM

Together the combination is a treat, but each partner in this recipe could stand alone or be combined with other things. Almond ice cream goes very well with chocolate, as does honey. Pears in wine sometimes serve as an accompaniment to roast partridge or pheasant.

Pears
4 PEARS
JUICE OF ½ A LEMON
1¾ PT/1 LITER LIGHT RED WINE OF GOOD QUALITY
1 CLOVE
1 TSP CINNAMON
3½ TBSP/1¾ FL OZ/50 ML GRAND MARNIER
7 OZ/200 G SUGAR
2 SLICES OF ORANGE
2 SLICES OF LEMON

Almond ice cream
13 TBSP/6½ FL OZ/195 ML MILK
1½ TBSP/¾ FL OZ/20 ML KARO/GLUCOSE SYRUP
1½ OZ/45 G SUGAR
1 DROP OF ALMOND EXTRACT

Garnish
4 CINNAMON STICKS

Preparation time: 1 hour (3 days marinating the pear)
Serves 4 people

Peel and core the pears and sprinkle with lemon juice. Place the remaining ingredients for the pear in a pan. Leave to simmer for 1 hour over a low heat. Take out the clove and transfer the liquid and pear into a dish and cover. Place in the refrigerator and leave the pears to marinate for two or three days, turning from time to time, to allow them to absorb the color of the red wine.

Mix all the ingredients together for the almond ice cream. Process in an ice cream maker. Once the ice cream is finished, place it in the freezer until ready to serve.

Place the pear in the center of a plate. Place a scoop of ice cream beside the pear and decorate with a cinnamon stick.

Chef's tip
It is best to use red wines, with light tannins such as Beaujolais, Chianti or Pinot Noir.

Sorbets Provençale

PROVENÇAL SORBETS

Mention Provence and the mind automatically conjures up thoughts of lavender, of wild thyme from the *garrigues* and the rose petal blush of *vin rosé*. Made into sorbets, they bring a fragrance and freshness to a meal, cleansing the palate, while bringing a summer meal to a perfect climax.

Lavender sorbet
¼ OZ/7 G LAVENDER (FRESH OR DRIED)
8½ FL OZ/250 ML MILK
2 TBSP/1 FL OZ/30 ML KARO/GLUCOSE SYRUP
2¼ OZ/60 G SUGAR

Thyme sorbet
¼ OZ/7 G THYME
8½ FL OZ/250 ML MILK
2 TBSP/1 FL OZ/30 ML KARO/GLUCOSE SYRUP
1 OZ/30 G SUGAR

***Rosé* wine sorbet**
10 TBSP/5 FL OZ/150 ML *ROSÉ* WINE
3½ OZ/100 G *ROSÉ* JELLY OR GRAPE JELLY
2 TBSP/1 FL OZ/30 ML KARO/GLUCOSE SYRUP
1 OZ/30 G SUGAR

Preparation time: 30 minutes plus the processing of the sorbet in an ice-cream machine
Serves 4 people

In a pot, steep the lavender in hot milk for 5 minutes. In a bowl, mix the remaining ingredients together and strain in the hot milk, making sure the sugar has dissolved. Process the mixture in an ice cream machine. Set aside in the freezer until ready to serve.

For the thyme sorbet, follow the same method used for the lavender sorbet.

For the *rosé* sorbet, mix together all the ingredients. Process this mixture in an ice cream machine. Set aside in the freezer until ready to serve.

Place a scoop of each sorbet on a plate. Garnish each scoop of sorbet with its corresponding flavor. Place a sprig of thyme on the thyme sorbet, sprig of lavender on the lavender sorbet, and for the *rosé* sorbet, place a small grape stalk with a few very small grapes.

Les ravioles au chocolat

CHOCOLATE RAVIOLI

Sweet pasta is often served as a dessert in France. This recipe is best made with any berries or fruit in season. Use the techniques in this recipe to experiment and make your own *ravioli* with your choice of filling.

Ravioli
¾ OZ/20 G SUGAR
¾ OZ/20 G BUTTER
1 PINCH OF SALT
¾ OZ/20 G BITTER CHOCOLATE POWDER
6½ TBSP/3½ FL OZ/105 ML HOT WATER
8¾ OZ/250 G WHITE FLOUR
2¼ OZ/60 G CORNSTARCH

Fruit mixture
2¼ OZ/60 G RASPBERRIES
2¼ OZ/60 G STRAWBERRIES
2¼ OZ/60 G RED CURRANTS
2¼ OZ/60 G MULBERRIES

Sauce
1 CARDAMOM POD/SEED
13 TBSP/6½ FL OZ/195 ML MILK
2 EGG YOLKS
1¼ OZ/40 G SUGAR

Preparation time: 50 minutes
Cooking time: 5 minutes
Serves 4 people

For the *ravioli*, dissolve the sugar, butter, salt and chocolate in the hot water. Add the chocolate mixture to the flour and work the ingredients together until a smooth paste is formed. Let this sit for 30 minutes. Mix the cornstarch together with some water; enough to make a paste like glue.

Process the pasta dough through a pasta roller/machine to form two thin sheets. Mix the fruit and berries together in a bowl, reserving a few for decoration. Lay out one sheet of the pasta, and place small spoonfuls of the fruit mixture at regular intervals. With a pastry brush, spread the starch mixture around the spoonfuls of fruit and place the second sheet of rolled pasta on top. Use your fingertips to gently press around the fruit. Cut out small rounds with a cookie cutter, either one large *ravioli* per person or smaller *ravioli* for several in each serving. Check each *ravioli* to be sure the edges are sealed. Set aside on a floured tray, and turn the *ravioli* from time to time. When ready to serve, poach in simmering water for 1–2 minutes and then drain on a paper towel.

To make the sauce, in a pot over a gentle heat, steep the cardamom in the boiling milk. In a bowl, cream together the egg yolks and sugar. Strain the milk into the egg mixture. Cook over a low heat, stirring constantly, until the mixture coats the back of a wooden spoon. Set aside.

Pour the sauce into a shallow bowl, place the *ravioli* on top and decorate with some of the remaining fruit.

Fondant au chocolat chaud

HOT CHOCOLATE FONDANT PUDDING

A *fondant* is known as a sugar syrup containing glucose, cooked to the "soft ball" stage, and then worked with a spatula until it becomes a thick opaque paste. Colored and flavored *fondant* is used in confectionary, to fill chocolates and sweets. Frédéric Rivière made this recipe at the *Auberge du Jarrier*, a restaurant where he once worked in Biot. This recipe is served in many French restaurants.

2¾ OZ/80 G FLOUR
3½ OZ/100 G DARK CHOCOLATE
3¼ OZ/90 G BAKING POWDER
5 EGGS
2¼ OZ/60 G BUTTER
1¼ OZ/40 G CASTER/BROWN SUGAR
13 TBSP/6½ FL OZ/195 ML FRESH WHIPPING CREAM, CHILLED
8½ FL OZ/250 ML VANILLA ICE CREAM

Preparation time: 15 minutes
Cooking time: 4–5 minutes
Serves 4 people

Break the chocolate into small pieces and allow it to melt in a *bain-marie*. Break the eggs into a separate chilled mixing bowl, add the sugar and beat. Pour in the melted chocolate and continue to beat briskly. Sift the flour and baking powder into a large mixing bowl. Slowly add the flour, a little at a time to the egg and sugar mixture, until incorporated. Grease a baking sheet with a bit of butter, and spoon four rounds of mixture onto the greased baking sheet. Bake in a preheated oven at 465°F/240°C for 4–5 minutes. While they are cooking, whip the chilled cream.

Place a spoon of the whipped cream in the center of four serving plates. When the *fondant* chocolates come out of the oven, place them on top of the cream. Place a scoop of ice cream at the side and serve immediately.

Chef's tip
Once portioned, the fondant mixture can be kept in the freezer.

La banane à la vapeur avec son coulis de mangue

STEAMED BANANA WITH MANGO COULIS

This is not a traditional French recipe, and the combination of bananas and mango is probably more Asian. The idea for this recipe was taken from the simple method of cooking vegetables by steaming them. The quality of the ingredients is very important to the final quality of this dish. The bananas should be ripe but not black or green. The mango should be soft but not overripe. Use the methods in this recipe to prepare other fruits in the same way. Steamed fruit is an excellent light and tasty dessert.

Bananas
4 BANANAS
2 SPRIGS OF MINT
¾ OZ/20 G CRYSTALLIZED ORANGE RIND
2 EGGS
3½ OZ/100 G SUGAR

Mango *coulis*
1 OZ/30 G SUGAR
4 TBSP/2 FL OZ/60 ML WATER
3½ OZ/100 G FRESH MANGO PULP
JUICE OF 1 LEMON

Decoration
FRESH MINT
RED BERRIES

Preparation time: 30 minutes
Cooking time: 5 minutes
Serves 4 people

Peel the bananas and cut them lengthways. Place the mint and orange rind in the middle, and close up the banana like a sandwich. Dip the banana into the beaten egg and roll in sugar. Wrap each sugared banana individually in plastic wrap and steam for 10 minutes.

In a pan, dissolve the sugar in water and bring to a boil. Allow cooling. Blend or process the mango pulp into the sugar mixture and add some lemon juice.

Place the *coulis* in the center of a plate. Remove the plastic wrap from the bananas (be careful, they will be very hot) and carefully place the banana on the *coulis*. Decorate with fresh mint leaves and red berries.

Chef's tip
Banana leaves can replace cling film/plastic wrap if you can obtain them (try your local Asian market).

Le fraisier

STRAWBERRY CAKE

Génoise is the sponge cake base of most *pâtisserie gâteaux* of which *le fraisier* is one of the best-known examples. As the name suggests it may have originated in Genoa around the start of the eighteenth century. Once the basic method has been learned, it can be adapted by the addition of ground hazelnuts, almonds, and coffee or, as here, chocolate.

Chef's tip
To obtain a multicolored sponge, divide the plain génoise/cake mixture (minus the chocolate powder) into two. Leave one part "natural" and add the chocolate powder to the remaining half. Using the wax paper, spread stripes of the batter, first one plain and then one chocolate. All the stripes should be connecting. Once cooked, cut two rounds from this to create a striped sponge cake.

Cake
2 EGGS
2¾ OZ/75 G SUGAR
2¼ OZ/60 G FLOUR
1 OZ/30 G UNSWEETENED CHOCOLATE POWDER

Mousse
2¼ OZ/60 G FRESH STRAWBERRY *PURÉE*/PULP
1½ OZ/45 G SUGAR
½ TSP/2 G POWDERED GELATINE/GELATINE LEAF
7 FL OZ/210 ML CREAM

Raspberry *coulis*
6¼ OZ/180 G FRESH RASPBERRY *PURÉE*/PULP
¼ OZ/7 G FRESH VANILLA
1½ OZ/45 G POWDERED CONFECTIONERY SUGAR

To flavor the cooked cake
2 TBSP/1 FL OZ/30 ML COINTREAU
4 TBSP/2 FL OZ/60 ML KARO/GLUCOSE SYRUP
STRAWBERRIES

Preparation time: 30 minutes
Cooking time: 8–10 minutes
Serves 4 people

Beat the eggs and sugar together in a mixing bowl until very light and fluffy. Carefully fold in the sifted flour and the chocolate powder, continue to stir until a smooth batter is formed. Spread the batter on a sheet of a wax paper in a circle, either eight small circles or two bigger circles (the same size as the ring mold you will use to assemble the cake). The mixture should be approximately ¼ in./7 mm thick. Bake in a preheated oven at 390°F/200°C for 8–10 minutes. Once cooked, set aside on a rack and cover with a dishcloth.

In a bowl, mix together the glucose syrup with the Cointreau. Take one of the large sponge cake rounds or four of the eight individual sponge cakes and dip them into the Cointreau and glucose syrup. Place the Cointreau-soaked sponge cake on the bottom of a large ring mold (or four small ring molds if making individual cakes). Place a row of strawberries around the side of the mold and fill the middle with the mousse mixture. Place the other half of the sponge cake on top. Refrigerate until ready to serve.

For the mousse, boil the fruit pulp and the sugar together in a saucepan. Pass the fruit pulp through a sieve to remove the seeds and set aside to cool. Next, soften the gelatine leaf in warm water or add just enough water to melt the powdered gelatine. Add the softened gelatine to the fruit pulp mixture and stir. Add the whipped cream before the pulp mixture begins to thicken.

For the raspberry *coulis*, mix together all ingredients in a blender, then strain and reserve.

Spoon some *coulis* into the center of each plate and place a piece of the large cake on top or one smaller individual cake on top.

Le soufflé glacé aux pruneaux et à l'armagnac

ICED PRUNE AND ARMAGNAC SOUFFLÉ

Prunes and *Armagnac* make one of the great culinary marriages, especially when they're served together in ice-cream form. The best prunes come from Agen in southwest France. *Armagnac* is produced in Gascony, mainly from the same ugni blanc grape as *Cognac*.

Soufflé
3¼ OZ/90 G SUGAR
3 EGGS
3 TBSP/1½ FL OZ/45 ML *ARMAGNAC*
2¼ OZ/60 G PRUNE *PURÉE*
4 TBSP/2 FL OZ/60 ML CREAM

Lace cookies
2¼ OZ/60 G BUTTER
2¼ OZ/60 G SUGAR
2¼ OZ/60 G BROWN SUGAR
2¼ OZ/60 G FLOUR
2¼ OZ/60 G ORANGE JUICE

Decoration
6½ TBSP/3½ FL OZ/100 ML WHIPPING CREAM
6½ TBSP/3½ FL OZ/105 ML CHOCOLATE (MELTED)

Chef's tip
It is a good idea to place the dessert glasses or dishes in the freezer 2–3 minutes before serving the soufflé – *this will make the dessert easier to cut.*

Preparation time: 15 minutes (30–45 minutes freezing time)
Cooking time: 5 minutes
Serves 4 people

In a pan, dissolve the sugar in a little water, just enough water to be absorbed by the sugar. Cook until the sugar mixture reaches 250°F/120°C on a candy thermometer. Separate the eggs and beat the egg whites in a large bowl until stiff. Remove the sugar from the heat and add the beaten egg whites to the sugar mixture and beat until completely cooled. Add the *Armagnac*, prune *purée* and beaten cream. To obtain the correct consistency, dip your thumb and index finger into a cup of cold water, quickly dip the two fingers into the mixture and then immediately back into the cold water, rub the mixture together in the two fingers; you should be able to work the mixture into a ball. Pour the *soufflé* mixture into individual *ramekins* and place in the freezer.

To prepare the lace cookies, melt the butter in a pan over medium heat or in the microwave. In a bowl, mix the remaining ingredients together and add to the melted butter. Drop spoonfuls of the mixture on a non-stick baking sheet at regular intervals allowing enough space for them to spread during cooking. Bake in a preheated oven at 355°F/180°C for 5 minutes. Let the cookies cool slightly, carefully remove from the tray and drape over a wooden spoon to gain the desired shape and leave until hardened.

Remove the *soufflés* from their molds and place on individual serving plates. Place the lace cookies around them and decorate with droplets of cream and melted chocolate.

La rondelle aux agrumes caramelisés

CHOCOLATE-COATED CITRUS MOUSSE
WITH A COULIS OF RED BERRIES

This is an amalgam of pastry techniques brought together to form a stylish composite dessert. Frédéric Rivière developed the idea by combining flavors, textures and methods he learned through his experience in some of the most celebrated kitchens of France.

Citrus fruit
1 ORANGE
1 GRAPEFRUIT
1 LIME
2 MANDARIN ORANGES

Mousse
3¼ OZ/90 G BUTTER
2¾ OZ/75 G *CRÈME FRAÎCHE*/SOUR CREAM
ZESTE OF 1 LIME
1¼ OZ/35 G GELATINE
2 TBSP/1 FL OZ/30 ML MANDARIN IMPERIAL LIQUEUR
5 EGG YOLKS
3½ OZ/100 G SUGAR
13½ FL OZ/400 ML WHIPPED CREAM

Icing
5¼ OZ/155 G COCOA BUTTER
10½ OZ/300 G UNSWEETENED BAKER'S CHOCOLATE
GOLD LEAF (IF AVAILABLE)

Coulis
7 OZ/200 G ASSORTED RED BERRIES
1 OZ/30 G POWDERED SUGAR
JUICE FROM 1 LIME
ZESTE OF 1 LEMON
6½ TBSP/3½ FL OZ/105 ML OF WATER

Decoration
4 FRESH MINT LEAVES

Preparation time: 30 minutes plus 45 minutes freezing time
Cooking time: 5 minutes
Serves 4 people

Wash and peel all the citrus fruits. Cut out the quarters of the fruit between the membranes.

For the mousse, melt the butter in a saucepan and add the *crème fraîche*/sour cream and lime *zeste*. Dissolve the gelatine in the mixture, add the liqueur and set aside. Beat together the egg yolks and sugar and add to the cooled sauce. Delicately fold in the whipped cream. Place the small bottomless stainless steel ring molds on a baking sheet. Fill each mold with the mousse and place in the freezer. When set, remove from the mold.

To prepare the icing, in a *bain-marie*, melt together the cocoa butter and chocolate. Let the mixture cool and spread on the frozen mousses. Place the chocolate-covered mousses on a plastic rack and decorate with the gold leaf. Place the finished individual mousses in the refrigerator to set.

Wash the assorted red berries. Blend or process the fruit together with the sugar, lime juice and the 6½ tbsp/3½ fl oz/105 ml of water. Pass through a fine sieve and add the lemon *zeste*.

Place a mousse in the center of a plate. Arrange the citrus fruits around the mousse. Pour a thin stream of the *coulis* around the plate and decorate with fresh mint.

Monder
Preparing tomatoes by removing the hull, slitting the bottom and plunging in to boiling water to remove the skin

Mortifier
To hang meat, poultry or game, in order to make it more tender

Mouiller
To add a liquid to something you are cooking

N

Napper
To coat or cover with sauce or aspic the prepared dishes

P

Paner
To egg and crumb any ingredients before frying

Pastis
An aniseed-flavored strong drink from the South of France; for example Pernod or Ricard

Pâtisserie
A French cake or pastry shop

Paysanne
A mixture of vegetables cut into small squares, used to make soups, garnish meat, fish, or omelettes

Peluche
Shreds of chervil or parsley

Persillade
A mixture of chopped parsley and garlic added to certain dishes at the end of cooking

Pincer
To color slightly in oven, vegetables, bones or chicken, before moistening

Piquer
To insert in meats or poultry *juliennes* of bacon fat, ham, truffle slices, garlic slices or herbs or a clove in an onion

Plat à sauter
A flat-bottomed pan with low sides

Pocher
To poach or to cook food in a liquid that is only slightly boiling

Purée
A creamy preparation obtained by pressing and sieving cooked foods (or by using a blender or food processor)

Q

Quenelle
An oval shape prepared with two spoons from a *purée*, mousse, ice cream or sorbet

R

Ragoût
A stew made from meat, poultry, game, fish or vegetables cut into pieces of regular size and shape and cooked with or without first being browned – in a thickened liquid, generally flavored with herbs and seasonings

Ramekin
A small round straight-sided *soufflé* dish, 4–4½ in./ 8–10 cm in diameter, in ovenproof china or glass; it is used to cook and serve individual portions

Ratatouille
A vegetable *ragoût* typical of Provençal cookery, originally from Nice. It is prepared with onions, zucchini, eggplants, sweet peppers and tomatoes simmered in olive oil with herbs

Réduire
To boil a sauce or stock, reducing it so as to give it a thicker consistency and more concentrated flavor

Repère
Flour mixed with water or white of egg, and used to seal lids of *cocottes* or pans when cooking

Revenir
To toss quickly in hot fat any meats, fish or vegetables in order to color them before moistening

Rissoler
To brown meat or potatoes in a pan in order to add color

Rouille
A Provençal sauce whose name describes its color, due to the presence of chillis and sometimes saffron

Roux
A cooked mixture of equal amounts of flour and butter, used to thicken many sauces

S

Sabayon
Egg yolk and wine whisked together over heat to form a creamy, stable emulsion. It's used to enrich sauces, or with added sugar, served as a dessert.

Saisir
To place food in a pan with or without oil or butter so as to sear its surface for extra flavor

Salamander
A gas apparatus for glazing items

Saucer
To pour sauce over or round a prepared article

Sauteuse
A *sauté* pan

Singer
To sprinkle with flour

Soufflé
A hot preparation which is served straight from the oven, so that it is well risen above the height of the mold in which it is cooked, but *soufflé glacé* is a frozen ice cream containing meringue

Suer
To place meats, fish, or vegetables in a pan with fat and heat slowly under cover

Suprêmes
A name given to the fillet or breast of fowl, fish, or game

T

Tamiser
To sieve food to make it as fine as possible

Tapenade
A condiment from Provence, made with capers, desalted anchovies, black olives pounded in a mortar and seasoned with olive oil, lemon juice, aromatics, and possibly a drop of marc brandy

Ten flavored pepper
Black, green, white, pink and Jamaican peppercorns, thyme, coriander, fennel seed, cardamon, and cumin

Tian
An earthenware cooking pot, which has come to refer to layered, baked dishes

Tomber des légumes
To cook vegetables with water and butter until the water is completely evaporated

Tournedos
A small round slice
½ in./1.5 cm thick, taken from the heart of a fillet of beef.

Tourner
To shape vegetables, using an appropriate knife, into specific regular form. Often this is a slightly rounded shape

Tronçons
Thick slices of fish or ox tail

Truffle
A subterranean fungus which lives in symbiosis with certain trees, mainly the oak but also the chestnut, hazel, and beech. The *truffle* is rounded, of variable size and irregular shape, and black, dark brown, or sometimes grey or white.

V

Velouté sauce
One of the basic white sauces, made with white veal or chicken stock or a fish fumet, and thickened with a white or golden *roux*

Voiler
To cover or surround certain pieces of confectionery with spun sugar

Z

Zeste
The yellow, glossy film or rind of an orange or lemon

Italian Cooking

Burned out candles in wicker Chianti bottles, red-checked tablecloths, rubbery pasta, mousetrap Parmigiano and phallic pepper mills – it is remarkable that our collective love affair with Italy managed to survive these unfortunate beginnings. Those early eating experiences now seem clichéd and rather comical, those obsequious, mechanically flirtatious waiters long gone; but out of that first, giddy flirtation has developed a more mature understanding of Italian food and culture. And it is in Tuscany, arguably, that the art of civilized living remains at its simplest and truest; the "heart" of Italy, *La Toscana*, is the Italy of our hearts. It is the vision that remains with us throughout the grey days. This is quintessential Italy, characterized by glorious inspirational landscapes from the Appennines to the Tyrrhenian Sea, great Renaissance cities, isolated hilltop towns and a love of good food.

Nowhere do the virtues of simplicity become more meaningful than in Tuscany; the irony is this rustic, robust cooking, once dismissed as plain and wholesome, is now recognized as a model of understated sophistication. The key to the flavor-driven, direct cooking, however, is ingredients, ingredients and ingredients. Freshness is all, and there is no place for any ingredient to hide that is less than absolutely fresh. Those feisty *nonnas* doing daily battle in the market place understand what freshness and quality really mean. For them, life is not too short to pick and choose their tomatoes by hand, to scrutinize the eyes and gills of fish, to sniff and prod the melons. It is what life is all about. Why give the people you love anything less than the best? Although life is changing in Tuscany, as convenience and junk food make inevitable inroads, it is a precept that still runs deep. And the land, rivers and sea of Tuscany still provide some of the best wine and food in Italy.

It used to be said that Tuscany has only three culinary virtues, beef, beans and Chianti – but, oh, what virtues! Beef from the distinctive, ancient cattle of the *Chiana* Valley to the southeast of Florence, is some of the most highly prized in the world. The small white beans or *fagioli* of Tuscany are eaten in soups, starters, main courses and as a vegetable dish in their own right. Two parts of the triumvirate come together in the dish of *fagioli nel fiasco*, rarely found these days, in which the beans are actually cooked in an empty Chianti wine flask.

Today, we would add to the list olive oil. Some of Italy's finest (and most expensive) oils come from Tuscany, as do so many wonderful classic and new wave "designer" wines, the *super-toscani*. We would add *salumeria* such as *Siense* sausages or *salame* made with fennel seeds and pork from pigs reared in the hill country; dense, crusty loaves of unsalted *pane toscano*, the perfect sourdough-style basis for *crostini*, *bruschetta* and *panzanella*; *panforte* from Siena and *cantucci* with *Vin Santo*, one of Italy's oldest sweet dessert wines. Tying these ingredients together would be the typical herbs of Tuscany – rosemary, sage and fennel.

Tuscan cooking is still rooted in a peasant and farming tradition, and every part of the food chain seems to connect to the pleasures of sitting, elbow to elbow, around a long table with family and friends. Its simple origins can be seen in original fast-food dishes such as *linguine alla vongole* and *crostini con i funghi*, as well as in the more complex preparations of *pappardelle sull lepre*, *pollo alla cacciatora* and *arrosto di maiale con fagioli all'uccelletto*.

The gastronomic journey to Italy should always begin – and perhaps end – in Tuscany, but the love affair now embraces the rest of the peninsula. *Carpaccio, bagna cauda, saltimbocca alla romana, zabaglione* and the like have transcended their origins and become for us part of the definitive Italian repetoire. Italian cooking has also evolved to take account of new ideas and new ingredients as the recipes for *farfalle al salmone affumicato* and *filetti di triglie servite con salsa di tapenade* show. Tuscany, like its cooking, remains the classical ideal – but as this unique collection of recipes by Giancarlo Talerico and Alvaro Maccioni shows, the "heart" of Italy is full and very welcoming.

Clarissa Hyman

Insalata mista di pomodoro e cipolla condita con olio di oliva e limone servita in un cestino di Parmiggiano

ORGANIC LETTUCE WITH TOMATO AND ONIONS IN A DRESSING ON A BASKET OF PARMESAN

If you want to impress your dinner guests, this is certainly the easiest way to do it. The basket of Parmesan will provide a healthy, tasty and crunchy start to your evening.

9 oz/250 g Parmesan cheese (grated)
7 oz/200 g mixed salad greens
3 fresh tomatoes
1 red onion

Dressing
1 tbsp/½ fl oz/15 ml balsamic vinegar
6½ tbsp/3½ fl oz/105 ml olive oil
1 lemon
Salt and ground black pepper

Preparation time: 20 minutes
Cooking time: 2 minutes
Serves 4 people

Warm a non-stick frying pan. Using the Parmesan cheese, you make four baskets. Sprinkle half of the cheese around the pan until you have a whole, large circle of cheese, to make each basket. When the cheese turns golden brown, it is ready. Turn the pan over onto a small bowl turned upside-down (base facing up). With a spatula, start to unpick the cheese beginning at the edges. Slowly it should fall over the upturned bowl. Leave to cool for a few minutes then gently separate from the bowl. This should form a basket of cheese.

Chop the tomato into cubes and chop the onion. Mix together in a bowl with the salad greens. In a cup, prepare the dressing by mixing the olive oil, lemon juice, balsamic vinegar, and salt and pepper. Pour the dressing over the salad and mix gently together. Place each basket on a starter plate then distribute the salad equally into each basket.

Chef's tip
This basket can be used for a cold appetizer. If you decide to use them with risotto, the Parmesan has to be mixed with corn flour to create a sturdier basket. Use ½ corn flour to ½ Parmesan. Use the finest quality Parmesan to ensure the basket takes.

Bruschette di pomodoro e basilico

TOMATO AND BASIL TOASTS

Bruschette and *crostini* are among the most common types of *antipasti*. The two are very similar and the terms often used interchangeably, but *bruschette* are generally larger and thicker. *Bruschette* means, "little burnt ones", and refers to how they should be prepared. Under a grill, whether charcoal or gas, or stovetop grill, the edges of the bread should be very crisp, and the center not too dry.

SLICED ITALIAN BREAD OR LONG LOAF OF FIRM-TEXTURED WHITE BREAD (CIABATTA TYPE)
4 VINE-RIPENED TOMATOES
1½ CUPS/340 G LOOSELY PACKED, FRESH BASIL LEAVES
2 GARLIC CLOVES (1 GARLIC CLOVE TO BE RUBBED OVER THE BREAD)
2 TBSP/1 FL OZ/30 ML EXTRA-VIRGIN OLIVE OIL
SALT AND PEPPER TO TASTE

Preparation time: 10 minutes
Cooking time: 10–15 minutes to toast the bread
Serves 4 people

Wash the tomatoes and chop into small cubes. Place the chopped tomato into a bowl and season with salt, pepper, olive oil, chopped garlic, and basil (torn into smaller pieces).

Toast the sliced Tuscan bread (or country loaf), which should be soft in the middle but crusty on the outside. Cut the toast into slices about 3 in./7.5 cm in diameter and ½ in./1.5 cm thick.

Toast the bread under the grill or charcoal oven until brown on both sides. For extra garlic flavor, rub a clove of garlic on the toast before spreading the tomato mixture.

Chef's tip
Be sure to tear the basil instead of chopping, as chopping blackens the leaves.

Fiori di zucca ripieni e fritti

DEEP- FRIED, STUFFED, ZUCCHINI FLOWERS

Zucchini flowers are a delicacy in Italy, but outside its boundaries, they may be difficult to find. First, begin with specialty retailers in your area and, if that proves unsuccessful, visit local farmers' markets. If you are able to procure the flowers, this unusual dish will reward your efforts. The best zucchini flowers are those that are still closed. As well as an *antipasti* dish, zucchini flowers may be served as a *contorni* accompanying fish or meat.

12 ZUCCHINI FLOWERS
3½ OZ/100 G *RICOTTA* CHEESE
1 OZ/30 G PARMESAN, GRATED
2 SPRIGS PARSLEY
7 OZ/200 G FLOUR
18¼ FL OZ/540 ML MILK
3½ TBSP/1¾ OZ/50 G BUTTER
SUNFLOWER OR OLIVE OIL FOR FRYING
SALT AND PEPPER
GREEN SALAD LEAVES

Preparation time: 15 minutes
Cooking time: 10 minutes
Serves 4 people

Prepare a batter by combining the flour, milk, butter, and a pinch of salt. Set aside. Prepare the filling by mixing the *ricotta*, Parmesan, chopped parsley and salt together.

   With a small spoon, place some of the cheese filling in the center of a zucchini flower. Carefully dip the whole flower into the batter mix and deep fry in hot oil until crisp and golden.

Serve warm on a bed of green salad leaves.

Melanzane alla parmigiana

EGGPLANT WITH PARMESAN

Sometimes referred to as *parmigiana di melanzane*, this is a classic and ubiquitous Italian dish. It probably originated in southern Italy, but its great taste and easy preparation has made it popular throughout Italy and a mainstay on the menus of America's Italian restaurants.

3 LB 5 OZ/1½ KG EGGPLANT
SALT
8 TBSP/4 FL OZ/120 ML OLIVE OIL
1 ONION
4½ LB/2 KG TOMATOES
3 FRESH BASIL LEAVES, TORN OR 2 TSP DRIED BASIL
FRESHLY GROUND BLACK PEPPER AND SALT TO TASTE
FLOUR FOR DUSTING
8½ OZ/240 G PARMESAN
5½ OZ/155 G MOZZARELLA
SPRIG FRESH ITALIAN PARSLEY

Preparation time: 40 minutes
Cooking time: 30 minutes
Serves 4–6 people

Trim the stems from the eggplant and slice into rounds. Sprinkle each slice with a little salt and place the salted slices in a colander. Cover with a plate and weight it down. Leave the eggplant to drain for 30 minutes.

To make the tomato sauce, heat four tablespoons of olive oil in a heavy pan and fry the onion until soft and golden. Add the skinned and chopped tomatoes and basil, mix well and simmer gently, uncovered, until the mixture reduces to a thick sauce. Season to taste with salt and pepper.

Rinse the eggplant slices thoroughly in cold water to remove the saltiness. Pat dry with paper towels and dust them with flour. Heat a little of the remaining olive oil in a large frying pan and fry the eggplant in batches, adding more oil as needed, until golden brown on both sides. Drain on paper towels. Oil a baking tray and make four to six stacks, alternating the eggplant slices, Mozzarella, and tomato sauce. Sprinkle each stack with Parmesan cheese and bake in a preheated oven at 390°F/200°C for 30 minutes. Serve hot, warm or cold.

Serve on individual serving plates with fresh Italian parsley and cracked black pepper.

Chef's tip

To make a lighter version, try grilling the eggplant slices.

Pasta fritta

DEEP-FRIED DOUGH

The Genovese love to snack on fried foods and there is a *friggitoria* or fried food stall on nearly every street corner. This typical dish, known as *pane fritto* or fried bread, uses pizza-like dough that can be dusted with either salt or sugar after cooking according to the mood of the moment.

8¾ oz/250 g white flour
½ oz/15 g fresh yeast
Water (enough to reach the desired consistency)
Sea salt
Ground black pepper
Olive oil for frying

Preparation time: 30 minutes
Cooking time: 20 minutes
Serves 4–6 people

Mix the flour, yeast, water and salt – until you arrive at a pizza/bread dough consistency. Work the dough for at least 20 minutes, then place it in a floured bowl and cover with a cloth.

Leave to rest in a warm place until it at least doubles in size.

Put the dough on a table, taking care not to touch it too often, otherwise, the air will escape from the mixture and it will start to shrink. With a spatula, cut away small pieces from the main mixture. The size of the pieces should be between 2½ in./6 cm long and ½ in./1.5 cm thick.

Place these pieces in a pan of boiling olive oil and fry until golden brown, making sure that you constantly turn the pieces. Once a golden brown, remove from the oil, drain on a paper towel, sprinkle with salt .

Arrange on a warm plate and serve as a warm appetizer.

Chef's tip
Try adding fresh herbs to the dough to add interesting taste variations.

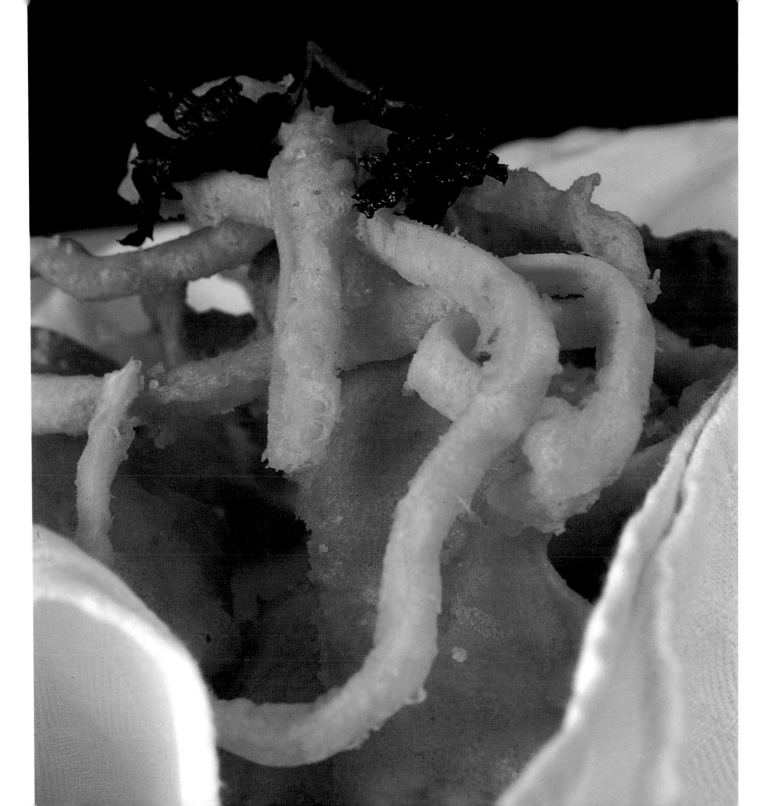

Polenta con fagioli

POLENTA WITH BEANS

Legume-loving Tuscans are nicknamed *mangiafagioli* (bean eaters), after the large number of Tuscan dishes that include beans. The white *cannellini* beans are the most closely associated with Tuscany.

1 LB 2 OZ/510 G FRESH *CANNELLINI* BEANS, SHELLED, OR 8½ OZ/240 G DRIED BEANS
6 TBSP/3 FL OZ/90 ML OLIVE OIL
3½ OZ/100 G *PANCETTA* OR BACON
2 GARLIC CLOVES
1 ONION
FRESH PARSLEY
1 TSP/5 G TOMATO *PURÉE* (PASTE), DILUTED IN 8 TBSP/4 FL OZ/120 ML OF COOKING LIQUID FROM THE BEANS
10½ OZ/300 G *POLENTA* (MAIZE/CORN FLOUR)
SALT AND FRESHLY GROUND BLACK PEPPER

To serve
EXTRA-VIRGIN OLIVE OIL
FRESHLY GROUND BLACK PEPPER

Preparation time: 2 hours (8–12 hours for the beans)
Cooking time: 2 hours 30 minutes (if using dried beans)
Serves 4 people

If using dried beans, soak overnight in plenty of water. The following day, drain and rinse, cook the beans in plenty of boiling water, until soft (approximately 1½ hours). Add salt towards the end of the cooking time. If using fresh beans, cook them in a large pot of lightly salted, boiling water until soft (approximately 35 minutes).

Heat the olive oil in an earthenware or heavy-based casserole dish and fry the onion, finely chopped garlic, chopped *pancetta* or bacon and parsley. Add the diluted tomato *purée* (paste) and simmer for several minutes.

Process the beans to a *purée*, add this bean *purée* along with their cooking liquid to the bacon and vegetables and season with salt and pepper. As soon as the mixture starts boiling, slowly add the *polenta*. Continue to cook for 35–40 minutes, stirring frequently to prevent lumps from forming.

Serve in individual bowls with bread. Have olive oil and freshly ground black pepper ready for guests to season their own beans.

Panzanella

TOMATO AND BREAD SALAD

Typical of its frugal Tuscan roots, *panzanella* was originally created as a way to make use of stale bread. It has become so popular, however, that it can be found throughout Italy, even in restaurants, and many people buy bread expressly to be used in *panzanella*. The ingredients for *panzanella* vary based on region. The addition of the cucumber, for example, is typical in and around Florence. Its refreshing qualities make it especially popular in the summer. Be sure to use a coarse, flavorful bread, and if the bread is not stale, toast it lightly before using.

1 LB 7 OZ/675 G ITALIAN BREAD OR FIRM WHITE BREAD, 2 DAYS OLD
6 RIPE, RED TOMATOES
8 ROMAINE/COS LETTUCE LEAVES
2 MILD RED ONIONS, PEELED AND SLICED
1 SMALL CELERY HEART, DICED
1 CUCUMBER
12 FRESH BASIL LEAVES, FINELY CHOPPED
½ GARLIC CLOVE, FINELY CHOPPED
3 TBSP/1½ FL OZ/45 ML RED WINE VINEGAR
6 TBSP/3 FL OZ/90 ML EXTRA-VIRGIN OLIVE OIL
SALT AND FRESHLY GROUND PEPPER

Preparation time: 1 hour 15 minutes
Serves 4–6 people

Cut the bread into thick slices. Peel and quarter the tomatoes. Scoop out the seeds and pulp and place in a bowl with the bread, which should be broken into small pieces. After the bread has absorbed the juice, add the skinned and quartered tomatoes. Next add lettuce cut into strips, onions, cucumber, celery heart, garlic and basil and carefully mix. Sprinkle the salad ingredients with the oil, vinegar, and season with salt and pepper. Cover the bowl and leave to chill for 1 hour in the refrigerator before serving.

Just before serving, sprinkle with a few drops of white wine vinegar.

Chef's tip
Dipping the tomatoes in very hot water (blanching) is the classic means to peeling. An alternative is to cut a cross at the top of the tomato and then gently rub the skin with the dull side of a knife. Pinch a corner of the cut between your thumb and the knife and pull. The skin should peel easily.

Focaccia alla erbe

FOCACCIA WITH HERBS

Focaccia, is slightly raised bread, similar to an undressed pizza base or crust, and is known all over Italy, but is particularly popular in Liguria, Toscana, Lazio and Umbria. Plain or with subtle added flavorings, it is widely appreciated as a snack throughout the region. *Focaccia* can also be served with fillings and is often served with a filling of fresh Mozzarella, lettuce and tomatoes.

14 OZ/400 G WHITE FLOUR
¾ OZ/20 G YEAST
½ OZ/15 G BROWN SUGAR
8½ FL OZ/250 ML WARM WATER
3½ TBSP/1¾ FL OZ/50 ML OLIVE OIL
½ OZ/15 G SALT
1 TBSP FRESH HERBS (ROSEMARY OR SAGE)
COARSE SEA SALT
FRESH BLACK OLIVES (APPROX. 20), SLICED

Preparation time: 2 hours
Cooking time: 20 minutes
Serves 4 people

Place the warm water, oil, salt and sugar in a bowl. Sprinkle over the yeast. Add the flour and combine to form a dough. If the dough is sticky, add more flour. When the dough is ready, make it into a mound and make a cross on the top with a knife. Leave the dough in a warm place for 1½ hours until doubled in size.
   Preheat the oven to 355°C. Flatten the dough with a rolling pin or by hand. Transfer to an oiled and floured baking tray. Leave the dough flat for 20 minutes. Sprinkle with olive oil, sea salt, fresh herbs and sliced fresh black olives. Place in the oven and bake for approximately 35 minutes.

Primi piatti

FIRST COURSES

From the term *primi piatti*, which literally means "first plates" of a meal, since *antipasti* are not always offered. The *primi* are most often a choice of pasta, *gnocchi* or risotto with modern menus now including *polenta*. Due to the peasant tradition of Tuscan cooking, soup is the more traditional of first courses in Tuscany (in the evening only), with almost all Tuscan soups being served over stale bread.

In Italy, pasta consumption is about 25 kilos/51 pounds, per person, per year. Pasta and its sauces are diverse and vary from region to region. For Italians, every pasta has a different taste and is split into three main categories: long pasta, short pasta, and fresh pasta each accompanied by its own sauce. Fresh pasta is made on the same day it is to be eaten. The type you typically find in the store is referred to as wet pasta, which should not be confused with fresh pasta (recipe for fresh pasta follows). Italians consider dried and fresh pastas to be simply different; each having their own virtues. In choosing a pasta, one should consider what sauce is to be used. Long pasta is generally used with sauces of fine/delicate consistency, while short pasta is better for thicker/chunkier sauces (see Pasta Glossary).

Pasta fagioli

THICK BEAN SOUP

Pasta fagioli is the most popular soup in Italy. For many years, during and after the Second World War, it was the main meal of the day for most Italians. It is usually served in the wintertime, hot, drizzled with a little olive oil, topped with Parmesan cheese and served with fresh homemade bread. The traditional recipe suggests cooking this dish in a crock-pot on a low setting for at least 3 hours.

¾ OZ/20 G TOMATO PASTE
5 OZ/10 TBSP/140 G SHORT PASTA (*DITALINI*)
10 OZ/20 TBSP/285 G *CANNELLONI* BEANS
1 SMALL ONION
1 GARLIC CLOVE
1 BAY LEAF
1 SPRIG SAGE
2 TBSP/1 FL OZ/30 ML EXTRA-VIRGIN OLIVE OIL
1 CARROT
1 STALK CELERY
1 TSP/5 G SALT
4½ PT/2½ LITERS WATER
OPTIONAL: BREAD

Preparation time: 1 hour (soak the beans overnight)
Cooking time: 2 hours
Serves 4 people

Soak the beans and sage overnight in cold water. The next day, drain the beans and rinse under cold running water. Chop the vegetables and garlic. Heat the oil in a deep pan, and *sauté* the vegetables for 5 minutes, while stirring occasionally. Add the bay leaf, the beans and the tomato paste. Stir for a few moments more and add the water. Cook for 1 hour stirring occasionally; when the beans are tender, it is time to season the soup and add the pasta. Remember, if the soup is too thick; add some more water to ensure the pasta is cooked properly. The pasta should take about 10 minutes.

Serve in individual bowls and sprinkle with extra-virgin olive oil.

Chef's tip
If using fresh beans, the recipe requires 1 lb 8 oz/700 g fresh beans and cook for 40 minutes. You can also cook the pasta separately and add to the soup.

Acquacotta

RUSTIC SOUP FROM MAREMMA

The Italian name of this sustaining, peasant soup literally means "cooked water" and is typical of coastal Toscana and upper Lazio (the *Maremma*), although the recipe varies widely from region to region. Here the vegetable soup is spiced with peppers and thickened with bread, cheese and eggs.

¼ LB/100 G PEPPERS
½ LB /200 G FRESH TOMATOES
3 TBSP/1½ FL OZ/45 ML OLIVE OIL
2 ONIONS, FINELY CHOPPED
2 STICKS CELERY, SLICED
4 EGGS
1¾ PT/1 LITER SLIGHTLY SALTED WATER
SALT AND PEPPER
2 TBSP PARMESAN
TUSCAN STYLE COUNTRY LOAF

Preparation time: 25 minutes
Cooking time: 20 minutes
Serves 4 people

Clean and seed the peppers. Dip the tomatoes in boiling water for several minutes, then peel and pass them through a sieve to obtain a *purée*. Heat the oil in a saucepan and fry the finely chopped onion until withered. Add the chopped peppers and sliced celery and simmer for 10 minutes. Add 1 liter of slightly salted boiling water and bring to a boil for approximately 5 minutes.

In a bowl large enough to contain the soup, beat the eggs and season with salt and pepper. Pour the soup over the eggs and sprinkle with Parmesan.

Place slices of toasted bread in warm serving bowls and add ladlefuls of hot soup.

Crema di patate con profumo di tartufo bianco

POTATO SOUP WITH A SCENT OF WHITE TRUFFLE

An old-fashioned soup with a modern twist; white *truffles* are highly prized in Italy for their incomparable, uniquely pungent scent.

½ MEDIUM, WHITE ONION
1 STALK OF CELERY
1 LEEK
2 TBSP/1 FL OZ/30 ML OLIVE OIL
3½ OZ/100 G SUGAR
4 POTATOES, DICED
13 TBSP/6½ FL OZ/180 ML MILK
1¾ PT/1 LITER CHICKEN STOCK
6½ TBSP/3½ FL OZ/105 ML WHIPPING CREAM
(OPTIONAL)
2 TBSP/1 FL OZ/30 ML *TRUFFLE* OIL
SALT AND PEPPER TO SEASON

Preparation time: 55 minutes
Cooking time: 45 minutes
Serves 4 people

Finely chop the onion, celery and leek, add to a pot with olive oil, and *sauté* for approximately 6 minutes. Add the sugar and salt and stir again for several minutes. Add the diced potatoes, milk and chicken stock, cook for 40 minutes, remove from the heat and blend in the whipping cream. Strain the soup and add half of the *truffle* oil, stir to combine and place in a serving bowl. Pour the remaining measure of *truffle* oil over the soup immediately before serving.

Serve in a bowl with *croûtons* and shavings from a fresh white *truffle*.

Chef's tip
Remember to preheat the bowls, and try adding a spoonful of sour cream to each bowl.

Minestrone

MINESTRONE SOUP

Minestrone actually means "big soup" and it is probably one of the most celebrated Italian soups. Although traditionally made from a variety of vegetables and pasta, and served with grated Parmesan cheese, there are hundreds of variations on this recipe.

4¼ oz/130 g white beans or *borlotti* beans
3 tbsp/1½ fl oz/45 ml olive oil
2 onions
2 garlic cloves
2¾ pt/1.7 liters water
4 tomatoes
2 carrots
2 potatoes
Diced turnip
1–2 celery sticks
8¾ oz/250 g cabbage
1¾ oz/50 g small pasta shapes (*ditalini*)
1 tbsp fresh parsley
Salt and freshly ground black pepper
3 tbsp grated Parmesan cheese and extra to serve

Preparation time: 30 minutes (8–12 hours for the beans)
Cooking time: 2 hours
Serves 6 people

Place the white or *borlotti* beans in a large bowl and cover with water. Leave to soak for 8 hours or preferably overnight. Drain the beans and rinse thoroughly under cold running water. Heat the oil in a large saucepan and add the chopped onions, crushed garlic and *sauté* gently for 5 minutes, stirring occasionally, until soft and golden brown. Add the beans, water, and skinned, seeded and chopped tomatoes, cover the pan and simmer gently for 1 hour, or until they start to be tender. Stir in the diced turnip, potatoes and carrots; cook for another 10 minutes. Chop the celery and shred the cabbage, and add these to the soup with the pasta. Cook for 10 minutes, or until all the vegetables are tender and the pasta is cooked.

Add the parsley and seasoning to taste. Stir in the Parmesan and then ladle into individual soup bowls. Serve immediately with extra Parmesan cheese and a drop of olive oil.

Chef's tip
To add an interesting flavor to the soup, try adding bacon along with the onions and garlic.

Zuppa pesce

FISH SOUP

Many of the less expensive or unattractive fish varieties can be used here and will provide surprisingly excellent flavor.

3¾ LB/1½ KG ASSORTED FISH (MULLET, SOLE, MANTIS PRAWNS, SHELLFISH)
4½ FL OZ/135 ML DRY WHITE WINE
1 LB 2 OZ/500 G *PURÉED* TOMATO/TOMATO PASTE
UNSALTED, STALE BREAD
2 GARLIC CLOVES
4 TBSP/2 FL OZ/60 ML OLIVE OIL
PARSLEY TO TASTE
POWDERED CHILLI PEPPER

Preparation time: 30 minutes
Cooking time: 1 hour
Serves 4 people

Clean and wash the fish if not already prepared. Brown the garlic in 4 tablespoons of oil in a large saucepan, add the powdered chilli pepper (the tip of a teaspoon) and add the white wine.

When the latter has evaporated, add the tomato paste and simmer for another 5 minutes over low heat. Add the fish, beginning with the variety needing the lengthiest cooking time and finishing with that needing the least. Continue cooking over medium heat for another 15 minutes, delicately moving the fish with the aid of a wooden spoon, so that the flavors of the sauce are absorbed well.

Toast some of the slices of bread and rub them liberally with garlic. Place one slice in each soup bowl, spoon over the *cacciucco*, smothering the toast in the "fish stock". Serve at once, with a sprinkling of parsley, if you wish.

Pasta fresca

FRESH PASTA

Many people are unnecessarily intimidated by making fresh pasta. With a pasta machine, pasta making can be surprisingly easy, and the result very rewarding.

This recipe can be used to make traditional spaghetti, hand-formed pasta, stuffed pasta, and sheets. The shape of the pasta should be compatible with the recipe. You can also experiment with variations in color and flavor by adding ingredients such as spinach, fresh herbs, tomatoes or beets.

The addition of the olive oil is optional. Olive oil gives the dough a smooth texture but can also make the dough harder to work. Experiment with and without the oil to decide which method you prefer.

If you are not using the dough immediately, cover with plastic wrap and refrigerate until needed. The dough will keep for up to three or four days in the refrigerator.

10½ OZ/300 G WHITE FLOUR (FLOUR SUITABLE FOR BREAD MAKING)
3 EGGS
2 TSP OLIVE OIL
SALT, 3 PINCHES

Preparation time: 50 minutes
Serves 4 people

There are two methods for mixing the pasta dough, by hand or with a food processor.

Mixing the pasta dough by hand
Pile the flour on to a clean work surface, make a well in the center and break the eggs into the well along with the olive oil and salt. Mix the flour, eggs, salt and oil together until dough is formed. Continue to knead the dough until you have a firm, smooth elastic texture.

Mixing the pasta dough by food processor
Put the flour, eggs, salt and olive oil into a food processor and blend until smooth. Roll the dough into cylinders and leave on a plate covered for 45 minutes to allow the dough to recover.

Pass the dough through a pasta-rolling machine at least 10 times to give you a very fine sheet of pasta.

Chef's tip
Salt is the secret to cooking pasta perfectly as salted water boils at a higher temperature. Use a good teaspoon of salt per liter of water. Salting the water not only helps the cooking but also seasons the pasta, which is not possible once the pasta is cooked.

Taglierini al gamberi freschi

PRAWN THIN NOODLES

This pasta and prawns recipe is typical of many found in coastal areas. The wonderfully light sauce subtly sets off the delicate taste of the fresh prawns.

Fettuccine (*taglierini*) PASTA TO SERVE 4 PEOPLE

Prawns
12 PRAWNS
4¼ OZ/120 G *CHANTERELLE* MUSHROOMS
1 OZ/30 G SHALLOTS
2 TBSP/1 FL OZ/30 ML OLIVE OIL
½ TBSP/7 G BUTTER
1 SPRIG OF THYME
1 GARLIC CLOVE
SALT AND GROUND BLACK PEPPER TO SEASON

Sauce
1¾ OZ/50 G LEEKS
1¾ OZ/50 G ONIONS
1 OZ/30 G CELERY
4 GARLIC CLOVES
3 SPRIGS OF PARSLEY
½ BAY LEAF
SALT AND BLACK PEPPER TO SEASON
13 TBSP/6¾ FL OZ/200 ML DRY WHITE WINE

To serve
⅓ BUNCH OF CHIVES
OLIVE OIL TO SERVE

Preparation time: 40 minutes
Cooking time: 45 minutes
Serves 4 people

Peel the prawns, keeping the flesh and shells. Finely chop the vegetables for the sauce, and place them in a saucepan, with the garlic, prawn shells, parsley, bay leaf and cracked pepper. Add just enough water to cover all ingredients, bring to a boil and continue to cook for 30 minutes. Be sure to remove impurities that appear on the surface. Strain the liquid and return to the heat adding the white wine, simmer until the liquid has reduced by half. This is now the prawn sauce.

Clean the mushrooms and place them in a dry frying pan with no oil and sweat until they release their own juice. Drain any juice that has accumulated in the pan.

In another frying pan, sweat the finely chopped shallots and garlic; add a half-tablespoon of butter and the *chanterelles*. Reheat the prawn sauce and check the seasoning.

Fry the seasoned prawns for approximately 1 minute in olive oil, garlic and thyme. Finally, in a pot of boiling, salted water, cook the pasta as directed.

Serve in a dish in the following order: the pasta, the *chanterelles*, the prawns, the prawn juice, finely chopped chives and a sprinkling of olive oil.

Pappardelle alla coniglio

PAPPARDELLE PASTA WITH RABBIT SAUCE

Although Tuscans are not generally known for their pasta dishes, this magnificent recipe dating back to the sixteenth century ranks amongst the best in the country. *Pappardelle* is slightly wider than *fettucine*, which can be used as a substitute.

1 RABBIT CUT IN PIECES
16½ FL OZ/490 ML DRY RED WINE
1 ONION
1 MEDIUM CARROT
½ STALK OF CELERY
1 SPRIG ROSEMARY
2 STEMS PARSLEY
8 WHOLE BLACK PEPPERCORNS
6 TBSP/3 FL OZ/90 ML EXTRA-VIRGIN OLIVE OIL
1 ONION
1 STALK CELERY
1 OZ/30 G BUTTER
14 OZ/400 G FRESH *PAPPARDELLE* PASTA
3½ OZ/100 G PARMESAN CHEESE
SALT AND GROUND BLACK PEPPER TO TASTE

Preparation time: 2 hours 15 minutes (5–6 hours marinating)
Cooking time: 2 hours
Serves 4 people

Wash the rabbit pieces thoroughly and pat dry with a paper towel. Place them in a large bowl with the wine, diced onion, diced carrot, diced celery, rosemary, parsley and peppercorns. Leave to marinate for at least 5–6 hours, turning several times.

Remove the rabbit from the marinade after the required time. Strain the marinade and reserve the liquid.

In a heavy pan, *sauté* the finely chopped onion and celery in the olive oil for 3–4 minutes over a moderate heat. Add the rabbit and cook over a slightly higher heat for approximately 5 minutes, turning the pieces to brown. Ladle some of the reserved marinade over the rabbit and bring to a boil. Cover and simmer over a low heat for approximately 1½ hours, turning the pieces occasionally and adding more marinade as needed.

Place the cooked rabbit pieces in a casserole dish to keep warm, strain the cooking liquid from the pan, pressing the vegetables through a sieve. Take three meaty pieces of rabbit from the center section, remove the meat from the bones and chop finely. Melt half the butter in a saucepan and add the sieved cooking liquid and chopped rabbit. Stir and leave to simmer for 10 minutes. Remove from the heat and stir in the remaining butter, the rabbit sauce and the Parmesan cheese. Meanwhile prepare the pasta and place the sauce on the pasta. Serve immediately.

Farfalle al salmone affumicato

SMOKED SALMON PASTA

A light creamy sauce such as this is the perfect accompaniment for the butterfly-shaped *farfalle*. This recipe is perfect made with fresh pasta. Using a fluted pastry wheel, cut a sheet of pasta into rectangles about 2 in./5 cm × 1 in./2.5 cm. Pinch the long sides of each rectangle together, creating butterflies or bow ties.

14 OZ/400 G *FARFALLE* PASTA
6¼ OZ/180 G SMOKED SALMON
1¼ OZ/40 G BUTTER
10 TBSP/5 FL OZ/150 ML HEAVY CREAM
3¼ OZ/90 G TOMATOES (OPTIONAL)
4 TBSP/2 FL OZ/60 ML FISH STOCK
BRANDY TO *FLAMBÉ*
CHOPPED PARSLEY
SALT AND FRESHLY GROUND BLACK PEPPER

Preparation time: 15 minutes
Cooking time: 20 minutes
Serves 4 people

Cut the smoked salmon into strips and gently *sauté* in the butter. Sprinkle a little brandy over the top and *flambé*. Add salt and pepper to season along with the cream and fish stock, continue to cook for another 5 minutes.

Cook the pasta separately in ample boiling, salted water until *al dente*, toss the pasta with the sauce and the cubed tomatoes (if using). Sprinkle with chopped parsley and serve.

Linguine alle vongole veraci

LINGUINE WITH CLAMS

Vongole veraci are the better of the two clams found in Italian seas. *Veraci* are larger, with a grey shell and a dark blue line down their center. For this sauce, many Italian chefs prefer to use dried/hard pasta such as spaghetti or *linguine*. Fresh pasta can also be used, but it will absorb more sauce than dried pasta.

14 OZ/400 G CLAMS
14 OZ/400 G *LINGUINE* PASTA
1 OZ/30 G BUTTER
2¼ OZ/60 G SHALLOTS, CHOPPED
1 GLASS DRY WHITE WINE
1 GARLIC CLOVE, CHOPPED
1 CHILLI PEPPER
2 TBSP PARSLEY
4 TBSP/2 FL OZ/60 ML OLIVE OIL
SALT AND BLACK PEPPER TO TASTE

Preparation time: 25 minutes
Cooking time: 15 minutes
Serves 4 people

Lightly *sauté* the chopped garlic and shallots and chilli in olive oil; add the clams and cook covered with a lid for 10 minutes. Add the white wine and 1 tablespoon of chopped parsley and continue to cook on a low heat for another 10 minutes. Add the butter and stir until melted. Season to taste with salt and black pepper.

Cook the pasta separately in boiling salted water until *al dente*.

Gently stir the clam sauce into the pasta and sprinkle with the remaining 1 tablespoon of chopped parsley.

Ravioli al basilico farciti con formaggio di pecora

BASIL RAVIOLI WITH FRESH GOAT CHEESE FILLING

Ravioli is popularly filled with minced meat, brains and chard or with fish. The addition of goats' milk cheese in this recipe is a French influence. You can add fresh basil leaves or other herbs to the basic pasta recipe to add further interest as you wish.

FRESH PASTA SHEETS (SEE FRESH PASTA RECIPE, P. 169)
15–20 FRESH BASIL LEAVES (OPTIONAL)

Ravioli filling
5¼ OZ/150 G FRESH GOAT CHEESE
2 SPRING ONIONS
SALT AND GROUND BLACK PEPPER TO TASTE
JUICE OF 1 LEMON
2 TBSP/28 G FLOUR WITH WATER (*ROUX*)
3 EGGS FOR SEALING THE PASTA

Garnish
CHOPPED SPRING ONION
OLIVE OIL
GRATED PARMESAN

Preparation time: 1 hour 30 minutes
Cooking time: 45 minutes
Serves 4 people

For the goat cheese filling, mix all ingredients together in a mixing bowl until fully combined.

Make the pasta dough according to the recipe. Run the pasta dough through a pasta machine once, lay flat on a board and place the fresh basil leaves on the pasta. Roll twice more through the pasta machine so the basil leaves are incorporated into the pasta sheet. Lay the pasta out flat and cut the large piece of pasta in half. On one piece of the pasta, at regular intervals, place teaspoonfuls of the goat cheese filling.

Beat the egg yolks with a few drops of water and brush it lightly around the small mounds of filling. Place the second layer of the pasta over the bottom sheet and press the two sheets of pasta together around the filling. Cut out *ravioli* shapes with a pasta cutter, either one large round *ravioli* per person or smaller individual *ravioli*. Cook the *ravioli* for 3 minutes in boiling, salted water with a drop of olive oil, strain immediately.

Place the *ravioli* on individual serving dishes garnished with grated Parmesan, chopped chives and a drop of olive oil.

Gnocchi di patate al pesto

FRESH POTATO PASTA WITH PESTO SAUCE

Gnocchi can be made from many ingredients but potato is by far the most popular. Take extra care when making as the potato makes them particularly delicate to handle.

For fresh potato *gnocchi*, it is better to use older potatoes, as they remain firmer. Boiling the potatoes in their skins keeps them drier, which makes the dough lighter. Pierce the potatoes as little as possible while cooking, and do not overwork the dough.

This is the basic *gnocchi* recipe and although it is teamed here with pesto sauce, try experimenting with your own flavors. Tuscans have taken to flavoring their *gnocchi* by incorporating ingredients like wild mushrooms and tomatoes.

Fresh *gnocchi*
10 OZ/300 G POTATOES
10 OZ/300 G WHITE FLOUR
1 TSP SALT
1 EGG, SLIGHTLY BEATEN (OPTIONAL)

Pesto sauce
SEE PESTO SAUCE RECIPE IN ITALIAN SAUCES
SECTION (P. 212)
PARMESAN
BLACK PEPPER
FRESH BASIL LEAVES

Preparation time: 45 minutes (including time to cook potatoes)
Cooking time: 2 minutes (for *gnocchi*)
Serves 6 people

Cook the potatoes whole with their skins in salted water until tender. Drain and peel, *purée* in a potato squeezer when hot. Place the potato *purée* in a large bowl. Add 1 cup of flour, salt and the egg. Knead with your fingers until smooth, adding more flour a little at a time until the dough is smooth and not sticky.

Separate the dough into 4 rolls, then cut into lengths of 1½ in./3 cm long and ½ in./1.5 cm thick. Take each small piece and press against the back of a fork so that one side will have the impression of lines and the other a small impression from your finger.

Place the *gnocchi* several at a time carefully into boiling salted water. The *gnocchi* are cooked when they float to the surface, which will happen quickly (1–2 minutes).

Once the *gnocchi* are cooked, strain and place in a bowl, fold the pesto mixture into the freshly cooked *gnocchi* and serve with freshly ground black pepper and extra Parmesan to taste. Garnish with fresh basil leaves.

Chef's tip
Try using sweet potatoes for an interesting taste variation. To make sure the gnocchi *works properly, mix the potatoes when they are hot.*

Risotto primavera

VEGETABLE (SPRING) RISOTTO

You don't have to be vegetarian to eat this great *risotto* full of fresh vegetables. Serve this tasty *risotto* on its own or as a substantial accompaniment to a main meat course.

1 LB 2 OZ/510 G *ARBORIO* RICE
2¾ OZ/75 G UNSALTED BUTTER
1 CARROT
1 ZUCCHINI
1 STICK CELERY
4 TBSP SHELLED FRESH PEAS
1 COS/ROMAINE LETTUCE HEART
SMALL AMOUNT OF ANY VEGETABLE TO ADD COLOR
2½ PT/1½ LITERS VEGETABLE STOCK (HOT)
SALT AND FRESHLY GROUND BLACK PEPPER TO SEASON
2¾ OZ/75 G PARMESAN CHEESE, GRATED

Preparation time: 40 minutes
Cooking time: 25 minutes
Serves 4–6 people

Melt the butter in a large heavy-based saucepan and fry the chopped vegetables gently for 5 minutes or until soft and translucent. Add the rice and stir until it is heated through and shining. Add the first ladleful of stock. Cook on a low flame and add more stock when the first addition has been absorbed. Continue in this way for approximately 20 minutes, or according to the time instructed on the packet, until the rice is swollen but still firm in the center.

Season to taste with salt and pepper, stir in the Parmesan cheese. Remove from the heat, cover and leave to stand for approximately 3 minutes.

Serve at once in warmed pasta bowls. Add a bit of grated Parmesan cheese and a drop of olive oil.

Chef's tip
Please read the cooking instructions on the risotto packet.

Risotto con la carne

MEAT RISOTTO

Add a sophisticated touch and a wonderful flavor to *risotto* with tender and juicy meat marinated in red wine and herbs.

12¼ OZ/355 G *ARBORIO* RICE
10½ OZ/300 G MEAT OF CHOICE
1 SMALL ONION, CHOPPED
1 STICK OF CELERY, CHOPPED
1 CARROT, CHOPPED
1 SPRIG OF ROSEMARY
2 FRESH SAGE LEAVES
1 GARLIC CLOVE, CHOPPED
BLACK PEPPERCORNS
1¾ PT/1 LITER DRY RED WINE
2¾ OZ/80 G BUTTER
1 TBSP/½ FL OZ/15 ML OLIVE OIL
1 LB 2 OZ/500 G FRESH RIPE TOMATOES, CHOPPED
14 OZ/400 G PARMESAN
1¾ PT/1 LITER BEEF OR CHICKEN STOCK (HOT)

Preparation time: 30 minutes (meat marinates 2 hours)
Cooking time: 1 hour 30 minutes
Serves 4 people

Dice the meat and lay it in a deep saucepan with the vegetables, herbs, garlic and peppercorns. Pour over the wine and cover the meat completely and leave to marinate for 2 hours.

Lift the meat from the marinade, reserving the liquid. *Sauté* it in a clean saucepan with a tablespoon of oil and half of the butter. Transfer the contents of the pan to a large pot, cover with the marinade and season. Simmer for half an hour, add the tomatoes and cook for another hour.

In the meantime, prepare the rice. Bring the stock to a boil. Put the other half of the butter in a deep saucepan and *sauté* the small onion until translucent. Tip in the rice and cover to the surface with the boiling stock. Cook until the rice is swollen but still firm in the center.

Check the seasoning and stir in the grated Parmesan.

Spoon the rice on a warm serving dish. Cover with the meat sauce and serve.

Chef's tip
Please read the cooking instructions on the risotto package.

Risotto ai funghi porcini

PORCINI MUSHROOM RISOTTO

This recipe relies on the famous porcini mushroom for its flavor. Outside of Italy, it may be difficult to find fresh porcini; cultivated mushrooms can also be used, while adding a little dried porcini for flavor. It is also possible to substitute porcini with other varieties of wild mushrooms such as chanterelles, oyster or morels.

14 oz/400 g *Arborio* rice
1 lb 2 oz/500 g fresh mushrooms
1 oz/30 g dried porcini mushrooms
½ onion
1 garlic clove
6 tbsp/3 fl oz/90 ml olive oil
1 leaf fresh sage
6 fl oz/180 ml dry white wine
2½ pt/1½ liters of vegetable or chicken stock (hot)
2¼ oz/60 g butter
2¾ oz/80 g Parmesan
Finely chopped parsley
Salt

Preparation time: 1 hour
Cooking time: 25 minutes
Serves 4 people

Place the dried porcini mushrooms in a bowl of cold water for several minutes until swollen, then slice.

Sauté the sliced onion and whole garlic clove in a pan with the olive oil, until the onion is translucent. Add the sliced porcini mushrooms and sage. Add the rice and white wine, allowing the wine to slowly evaporate. Cook on a low flame and adding a ladleful of stock at a time, add more stock when the first addition has been absorbed. Continue in this way for approximately 20 minutes or until the rice is swollen but still firm in the center.

Once cooked, remove the rice from the heat, take out the sage and garlic clove, and stir in the grated Parmesan, butter, and finely chopped parsley. Serve immediately.

Chef's tip
Please read the cooking instructions on the risotto packet.

Risotto al tartufo

TRUFFLE RISOTTO

Along with pasta and *polenta,* rice is a staple for Italians who have developed a unique way to prepare it. Though the essence of risotto is very basic, it is capable of absorbing a multitude of flavors. Despite the varying ingredients used, the techniques for making risotto are nearly always the same; not difficult but require patience and attention. This recipe relies on the famous white *truffle* for its flavor. Outside of Italy, it may be difficult to find, but *truffle* oil can be used as a substitute.

14 OZ/400 G *ARBORIO* RICE
3 OZ/80 G PARMESAN CHEESE, GRATED
2½ PT/1½ LITERS CHICKEN OR VEGETABLE STOCK (HOT)
2 OZ/50 G BUTTER
6 FL OZ/180 ML DRY WHITE WINE
6 TBSP/3 FL OZ/80 ML OLIVE OIL
½ ONION
1 WHITE *TRUFFLE*/5 FL OZ/150 ML *TRUFFLE* OIL

Preparation time: 1 hour
Cooking time: 25 minutes
Serves 4 people

Heat the oil in a large pan. Add the chopped onion and *sauté* until it browns. Add the rice and stir for a minute; add the wine and simmer until the wine has been absorbed. Gradually add the stock, a little at a time, so the mixture keeps a creamy consistency. Stir at all times and keep adding stock until the rice is cooked. This should take about 20 minutes depending on the packet instructions. Remember it should be *al dente* but not hard. Do not overcook or it will become soggy. When cooked, remove from heat and stir in the Parmesan and butter.

Serve immediately in a warmed bowl with finely shaved *truffle* or the oil on the top.

Chef's tip
Please read the cooking instructions on the risotto packet.

Gorgonzo la risotto

RISOTTO WITH GORGONZOLA

The very strong taste of good ripe Gorgonzola is unmistakable and absolutely delicious. If you find it a little too strong, try using half the quantity or alternatively use Dolcelatta, which is younger than Gorgonzola by about six months but still the same cheese. Incidentally, Dolcelatta is only made for foreign export. Follow this risotto with a mouth-cleansing *rocket*/arugula salad with orange.

1 ONION CHOPPED
3½ OZ/100 G UNSALTED BUTTER
14 OZ/400 G RISOTTO RICE
2 PT/1.2 LITERS CHICKEN OR VEGETABLE STOCK (HOT)
3½ OZ/100 G RIPE GORGONZOLA CHEESE
2 TBSP CREAM
4 FRESH SAGE LEAVES, VERY FINELY CHOPPED
SEA SALT AND FRESHLY GROUND BLACK PEPPER
6 FRIED SAGE LEAVES TO GARNISH
FRESHLY GRATED PARMESAN CHEESE TO SERVE

Preparation time: 30 minutes
Cooking time: 25 minutes
Serves 4 people

Fry the onion and half the butter until the onion is soft and melting but *not* browned. Add all the rice and raise the heat slightly to toast the grains, stirring so that they are covered with onion and butter. Don't let any of the ingredients brown, but make sure you get the rice really hot before adding the first ladleful of stock. Begin to add the hot stock, stirring constantly and allowing the liquid to be absorbed before adding more.

When you have added half the stock, stir in the Gorgonzola cheese. It will melt quickly and soon become distributed throughout the rice if you keep stirring. Continue to cook the rice, making sure that the grains always absorb the stock before you add more liquid. This will take about 20 minutes in all. When the risotto is creamy and velvety, but the rice grains are still firm to bite, remove from the heat and stir in the remaining butter, the cream and the fresh sage.

Adjust the seasoning; bearing in mind that Gorgonzola is very salty, so you will probably like a little pepper. Cover and leave to rest for 2 minutes.

Turn out on to a warm platter, garnish with the fried sage leaves and serve at once with the Parmesan cheese offered separately.

Risotto ai frutti di mare

SEAFOOD RISOTTO

The Italians have a great love of fresh seafood. Here we have a recipe to make a great dish for Italians and all seafood lovers. Although rice is a basic food for almost three-quarters of the world's population, we present to you a whole new way of marrying rice and seafood together.

Risotto
3½ OZ/100 G *ARBORIO* RICE
¾ OZ/25 G ONION
1½ FL OZ/45 ML DRY WHITE WINE
1 FL OZ/30 ML OLIVE OIL
8½ FL OZ/250 ML FISH STOCK (HOT)
3 SMALL CLOVES OF GARLIC

To accompany the rice
3½ OZ/100 G CLAMS
3½ OZ/100 G MUSSELS
1 CALAMARI
4 LANGOUSTINES
4 SCALLOPS
1¾ FL OZ/50 ML DRY WHITE WINE
1 CLOVE OF GARLIC

Seasoning
SALT AND PEPPER

Preparation time: 1 hour
Cooking time: 20–25 minutes
Serves 4 people

Scrub and wash the clams and mussels. To open the shells, heat the oil in a pan, add the garlic and the shells together; add the white wine. Cover the pan for a few minutes. Open the shells and scoop out the flesh, put to one side and retain the juice. Shell the langoustines, leaving the head and the tail. Prepare the scallops by taking them out of their shells and separating the fleshy part. Wash and pat dry thoroughly. Wash the calamari, remove the skin and cut into hoops. Heat the oil in a pan, add the scallops, then the langoustines and calamari and cook for a few minutes. Add the wine and reduce. Leave to the side.

To prepare the risotto, peel and finely chop the onion and garlic. *Sauté* with olive oil. Add the rice and cook for 1 minute until it becomes translucent. *Déglacer* with white wine and reduce until dry. Cover the rice with half the fish stock (see Stocks in the French section, p. 93). This should absorb in 8–10 minutes cooking on a low flame. As and when the first addition has been absorbed, add the rest of the stock. Stir the rice and stock continuously until the stock has been almost completely absorbed (approximately another 8–10 minutes). At this time, add the fish and stir together. Cook together for another 2 minutes. The total cooking time will be around 20 minutes, at the end of which the rice should be *al dente*. Season with salt and pepper.

Serve in warm bowls and drizzle a little olive oil over the top. If you prefer, you can cook the risotto by itself and then add the cooked fish to the top of the rice to make a different presentation, or you can add a few spoonfuls of fresh tomato sauce into the rice to give a nice color and flavor to the dish.

Chef's tip
Always read the instructions on the risotto packet because many have different cooking times.

Secondi piatti

MAIN COURSES

The *secondo piatto* is the main course of a meal, usually based on meat, fish or poultry, and often accompanied by vegetables or salad.

In its use of meat, Italian cuisine differs from that of many Western countries. While the meat, fish or poultry may be the focal point of a meal; it is understood to be but one part of the whole. Because the meal will typically also include soup, pasta or rice, perhaps an *antipasto* to begin, as well as fruit and cheese to finish, the meat is often in small portions, frequently used primarily for flavor. Of course, there are also the spectacular dishes such as *arista di maiale* – a pork loin known as "the best" – and the famous *bistecca alla Fiorentina* – Italy's most prized T-bone – which we present served with *rucola*.

Arrosto di maiale

ROAST PORK

This recipe is based on the well-known Tuscan dish of *arista*, roasted pork loin. The history of this dish dates back to Renaissance time when the difficulties of travel meant that hosts could never be sure at what time guests would arrive. As a result, they prepared dishes which would last for some time, and the natural preservative qualities of rosemary, pepper and garlic mixed with plenty of salt not only helped the meat to stay fresh but also provided a mouth-watering smell.

4 × 4¼ OZ/130 G LOIN PORK CHOPS
2 GARLIC CLOVES, SLICED
1 SPRIG OF FRESH ROSEMARY
4 SAGE LEAVES
SALT AND FRESHLY GROUND BLACK PEPPER
4¼ OZ/120 G *PANCETTA* OR SLICED BACON
BUTTER

Preparation time: 10 minutes
Cooking time: 40 minutes
Serves 4 people

Prepare the pork chops by breaking the points off the bones. Pierce the meat with a sharp thin-bladed knife and insert into the holes the sliced garlic cloves, rosemary leaves and sage leaves. Season to taste with salt and pepper.

Wrap the chops in *pancetta* rashers and place them in a buttered ovenproof dish. Bake in a preheated oven at 355°F/180°C for approximately 40 minutes.

These pork chops are traditionally served with beans.

Osso buco alla Milanese

BRAISED SHIN/SHANK OF VEAL

Osso buco (literally bone and hole) is braised shin or knuckle of veal traditionally cooked *alla milanese*, i.e. stewed very slowly for a long time. There are several variations on this basic theme, but everyone agrees the best bit is the veal marrow – scoop it out with a long-handled spoon. It is usually served with a *gremolada* and accompanied by saffron risotto.

4 SHIN OF VEAL
FLOUR FOR DUSTING
1 ONION, CHOPPED
1 CARROT, THINLY SLICED
1 CELERY STICK, THINLY SLICED
1 TBSP/15 G TOMATO PASTE
SALT AND FRESHLY GROUND BLACK PEPPER
2–3 SAGE LEAVES
1 SPRIG ROSEMARY
1 CLOVE GARLIC
10 TBSP/5 FL OZ/150 ML DRY RED WINE
3½ TBSP/1¾ FL OZ/50 ML OLIVE OIL
1¾ PT/1 LITER VEAL/VEGETABLE STOCK

Gremolada
4 TBSP/56 G FINELY CHOPPED PARSLEY
1 GARLIC CLOVE
1 ANCHOVY FILLET
ZESTE FROM ½ A LEMON
2 TSP/10 G BUTTER

Preparation time: 30 minutes
Cooking time: 1½–2 hours
Serves 4 people

Season the veal and pass with flour on each side and *sauté* in a pan for 5 minutes turning several times until they are golden brown on all sides. In a shallow frying pan, *sauté* the chopped onion and garlic until they are soft and golden. Add the thinly sliced carrot, celery, sage leaves, rosemary and veal. Season with salt and pepper and add the tomato paste, add the wine, and cook until it is completely absorbed. Cover the pan with the stock and simmer gently for approximately 1 hour, or until the veal is cooked and tender. Add a few tablespoons of stock if the sauce evaporates too quickly.

While the veal is cooking, prepare the *gremolada*. Mix together thoroughly the parsley, garlic, anchovy and lemon *zeste* until well combined. Spread each piece of veal with a little of the *gremolada* and cook 5–10 minutes. Transfer the veal to a heated serving dish and keep warm. Add a few tablespoons of water to the pan juices and bring to a boil, scraping the bottom of the pan clean. Simmer until slightly reduced and thickened. Stir in the butter; and when it has melted, pour over the veal.

Saltimbocca alla romana

VEAL ESCALOPES WITH PARMA HAM AND SAGE

Saltimbocca means "jump in your mouth", and the flavor of this beautiful dish explains how it got its name. Often the veal is rolled but here as an alternative, it is presented flat. In Italy, the cured ham (*prosciutto*) that comes from Parma is prized as much as the famous Parmesan cheese made nearby. Parma ham is preferred, but any cured ham is acceptable – just be sure you buy it uncooked.

12¼ oz/350 g veal escalope/thin slices
without any bone
6 Parma ham slices
4 fresh sage leaves, chopped
8 oz/230 g white flour

Garnish
4 sprigs fresh sage
3½ tbsp/1¾ fl oz/50 ml olive oil
Black pepper
7 oz/200 g mixed lettuce

Preparation time: 20 minutes
Cooking time: 2–3 minutes
Serves 4 people

Slice the veal very finely, allowing three slices per person. Dust with the flour, and place the dusted veal on an oiled baking tray. Place a piece of the Parma ham on each veal escalope and sprinkle with a little of the chopped sage. Prepare and thoroughly dry the lettuce and place in a salad bowl.

Preheat the oven to 430°F/220°C. Season the salad and pour over your choice of dressing. Put a little salad in the center of each plate. Cook the meat for approximately 1 minute in the oven and remove and arrange the pieces immediately around the salad. Pour some of the cooking juices over each veal escalope and garnish with fresh sage leaves and serve.

Chef's tip
You may substitute sliced chicken or turkey breast for the veal. Additionally, placing a slice of mozzarella adds richness.

Salsicce e fagioli

SAUSAGES WITH BORLOTTI BEANS

The celebrated Siense pork makes fabulous sausages. For authenticity, use real pork sausages without fennel seeds or hot pepper. This dish makes a hearty meal in itself and is especially good on cold winter evenings.

1 LB 2 OZ/500 G FRESH *BORLOTTI* BEANS, SHELLED
8¾ OZ/250 G DRIED BEANS SUCH AS *CANNELLINI*
3½ TBSP/1¾ FL OZ/50 ML OLIVE OIL
2 GARLIC CLOVES
1 ONION
1 CELERY STICK
1 CARROT STICK
2 TBSP/1 OZ/30 G CHOPPED FRESH PARSLEY
1 TBSP/14 G TOMATO *PURÉE* (PASTE), DILUTED IN
4 TBSP/2 FL OZ/60 ML WARM WATER
12 ITALIAN SAUSAGES, WITHOUT FENNEL SEEDS
SALT AND FRESHLY GROUND BLACK PEPPER

Preparation time: 2 hours (soak the beans overnight)
Cooking time: 2 hours 15 minutes
Serves 6 people

Soak the *cannellini* beans overnight in cold water. Next day, rinse the beans and cover with fresh water. Bring to a boil and boil for 5 minutes. Drain and rinse, cover generously with fresh water and simmer slowly for approximately 45 minutes, or until the beans are tender.

Shell the fresh beans and boil in plenty of slightly salted water for approximately 35 minutes.

Heat the olive oil in a frying pan (skillet) with the chopped garlic, onion, celery, carrot and parsley until all the vegetables are soft. Finally add the tomato *purée* (paste). Stir together thoroughly; then add the sausages. *Sauté* together for several minutes.

Add the fresh and dried beans and their liquid. Season to taste with salt and pepper. Simmer covered together for 30 minutes, until thickened and rich, like a stew. Serve warm.

Chef's tip

If short on time, use a tin of high-quality canned cannellini beans.

Pollo alla cacciatora con polenta

CHICKEN WITH POLENTA

Alla cacciatora means "cooked the hunter's way" but it does not denote a particular cooking method. Until the postwar years, chicken in most parts of Europe was reserved for special occasions; it was much too valuable, for the eggs it produced, to be eaten casually. However, a tradition was developed that hunters, on the eve of their hunt, would order a chicken cooked in a simple sauce as fuel for their coming hunt – hence the name of this dish.

1 WHOLE CHICKEN, PREFERABLY FREE RANGE
FLOUR FOR DUSTING
2 CARROTS
2 CELERY STICKS
1 MEDIUM ONION
1¾ PT/1 LITER CHICKEN STOCK
6 FL OZ/180 ML DRY WHITE WINE
3½ OZ/100 G MIXED, FRESH MUSHROOMS
2 OZ/55 G DRIED PORCINI MUSHROOMS
1 GARLIC CLOVE
1 TBSP/½ FL OZ/15 ML OLIVE OIL
BOUQUET OF ROSEMARY AND SAGE
14 OZ/400 G CRUSHED OR CHOPPED TOMATOES
1 OZ/30 G TOMATO PASTE
SALT, BLACK PEPPER AND NUTMEG TO TASTE

Preparation time: 1 hour
Cooking time: 1 hour 30 minutes
Serves 4 people

Cut the chicken into eight pieces (divide each breast in two and separate the thigh from the drumstick). Remove the skin, season with salt and pepper and dust with flour and set aside.

Place the chicken pieces in a pot of boiling salted water with one chopped carrot, half an onion, one stick of celery and boil together, simmer for 1 hour.

Place the dried mushrooms in a bowl of water until you need them. Strain the mushrooms in a sieve before using. Cut the vegetables into a *julienne* and *sauté* with olive oil in a pot for several minutes. Add the seasoned and floured chicken pieces and *sauté* on both sides until done, next add the porcini mushrooms and the wine. When the wine has evaporated, add the crushed tomatoes and tomato paste. Add the chicken stock through a strainer and continue to cook for 30 minutes.

Serve over the *polenta* (see *polenta* recipe in the *Contorni* section p. 224).

Bistecca alla Fiorentina con rucola

SLICED FLORENTINE STEAK WITH ROCKET/ARUGULA

Bistecca alla Fiorentina is the most famous steak in Italy and ideally should be made with prized chianina beef, from the beef of the *Val di Chiana*. Their meat has a remarkable combination of leanness, tenderness and full flavor. The T-bone steaks, weighing around 1½ lb/750 g per portion, need no marinating and are cooked without butter or oil over a real charcoal or wood ash fire. The steak should be eaten rare.

2 (1¾ LB/800 G) T-BONE OR PORTERHOUSE STEAKS
7 OZ/200 G FRESH *RUCOLA*/ARUGULA
3½ TBSP/1¾ FL OZ/50 ML OLIVE OIL
SALT
GROUND BLACK PEPPER TO SEASON

Preparation time: 10 minutes
Cooking time: approx. 20 minutes depending on preference
Serves 4 people

Preheat the grill until there is no longer any flame, just wood or charcoal ash. Place the steaks on the grill 4 in./10 cm from the glowing embers. Cook on each side for 4 or 5 minutes, or until a brown crust forms. Sprinkle the seared surface of the steak with a little salt, turn, and cook the other side, sprinkling again with salt and a little more pepper. In true Florentine style, the steaks should be well browned and sealed on the outside, rare and juicy on the inside.

Slice the steak and transfer to a serving plate. Top with the fresh *rucola*/arugula and season. Sprinkle with a little olive oil if desired.

Chef's tip

Ask the butcher to cut the steaks three inches thick and to include a section of fillet and contra fillet in each one. Each 1¾ lb/800 g steak should serve two people.

Polipi in padella

OCTOPUS WITH GARLIC SAUCE

"I had a friend named Tito whose family used to come and stay with us in early spring. In the summer, we would return the visit and go to stay in their house in Viareggio. Tito's mother used to make this dish using the octopus she had brought fresh from the market that morning."

Alvaro Maccioni

1 LB 2 OZ/500 G SMALL OCTOPUS
2 GARLIC CLOVES
1 TBSP FRESH PARSLEY
6 TBSP/3 FL OZ/90 ML OLIVE OIL
SALT AND PEPPER
1 LEMON

Preparation time: 20 minutes
Cooking time: 20 minutes
Serves 4 people

Peel off as much as possible of the octopus outer skin, and cut out the eyes and the mouth opening and yellow sack. Wash the octopus in plenty of running water and cut into thick ribbons.

Put the olive oil in a frying pan and *sauté* the finely chopped garlic and parsley. Add the octopus, stir for 2–3 minutes, season with salt and pepper, cover and simmer for approximately 15 minutes.

Serve hot, garnished with lemon slices.

Chef's tip
Choose a small octopus, as it is easier to prepare.

Branzino in cartoccio

SEA BASS BAKED IN A BAG

Cooking fish in a bag is a favorite Tuscan technique. This recipe never fails to impress, and no one needs to know how easy it is to prepare. When it is presented at the table, the appearance of the sealed bag and the aroma when it is opened before your guests will be sure to impress.

4 SEA BASS
4 SMALL POTATOES
3 SMALL TOMATOES
1 ONION
½ CUP LOOSELY PACKED BASIL LEAVES
OLIVE OIL
COARSE SEA SALT
FRESHLY GROUND BLACK PEPPER

Preparation time: 30 minutes
Cooking time: 20 minutes
Serves 4 people

Thinly slice the potatoes and place two layers at one end of a large piece of aluminum foil. Thinly slice the onion and place this on top of the layers of potato. Clean the fish fillet (two fillets per fish) and put a fillet on top of each of the potato-and-onion portions. Top with cubed tomatoes, basil, drizzle with olive oil, and season with salt and pepper. Fold one end of the tin foil over the other and seal the edges tightly into the shape of a fish. Cook in the oven for 20 minutes at 390°F/200°C.

Leaving the fish in the foil, place on a plate and serve with a green side salad.

Tonno fresco alla marinara

FRESH TUNA WITH TOMATOES

Of the countless preparations for tuna that can be found in coastal towns in Tuscany, this is the most popular. This recipe comes from Livorno, a populous port famous for its seafood restaurants.

4 FRESH TUNA STEAKS (APPROX. 5¼ OZ/155 G EACH)
SALT AND FRESHLY GROUND BLACK PEPPER
FLOUR FOR DUSTING
3½ TBSP/1¾ FL OZ/50 ML OLIVE OIL
1 ONION
2 GARLIC CLOVES
1½ LB/700 G TOMATOES, FRESH, PEELED AND CHOPPED
2 TBSP FRESH PARSLEY
4 BASIL LEAVES
1 BAY LEAF
4 ANCHOVY FILLETS, MASHED
8 BLACK OLIVES

Preparation time: 30 minutes
Cooking time: 30 minutes
Serves 4 people

Wash the tuna steaks and pat dry with paper towels. Season with salt and plenty of freshly ground black pepper, then dust the steaks lightly with flour. Heat half of the olive oil in a large shallow frying pan and *sauté* the tuna steaks until golden on one side. Turn and cook the other side until golden. Carefully remove the tuna steaks from the pan and transfer to a dish and keep warm. Add the remaining oil to the pan and *sauté* the chopped onion and garlic for approximately 5 minutes, until golden and soft. Add the tomatoes, parsley, basil, bay leaf and mashed anchovies and stir well. Bring to a boil and continue boiling until the mixture reduces and thickens.

Return the tuna to the pan, season to taste and simmer gently for 15 minutes, turning once. Remove the pan from the heat and add the olives and leave to stand for 5 minutes. Discard the bay leaf and transfer the tuna steaks in their sauce to a warm serving dish.

Chef's tip
Dice sun-dried tomatoes and fresh basil for decoration around the tuna.

Triglie alla Maremmana

RED MULLET – MAREMMANA STYLE

This is a typical plate from Maremmana, one of the most beautiful places in southern Italy; its beauty is reflected in this dish, and this is why we call it "Maremmana". The unusual part about this plate is the use of fish and *prosciutto* together to create a twist in the flavor with outstanding results.

1 LB 6 OZ/800 G RED MULLET/RED SNAPPER
3½ OZ/100 G *PROSCIUTTO CRUDO*, FINELY MINCED
2 TBSP/1 FL OZ/30 ML OLIVE OIL
JUICE OF ½ A LEMON
1 GARLIC CLOVE, MINCED (GROUND)
SALT AND FRESHLY GROUND BLACK PEPPER
FRESH WHITE BREADCRUMBS, FOR COATING
4 OZ/120 ML DRY WHITE WINE
1 TSP/5 G BUTTER

Preparation time: 2 hours
Cooking time: 15 minutes
Serves 4 people

Clean and gut the fish, wash them in plenty of running water and leave to drip for a few minutes. Finely mince the *prosciutto crudo*. Stuff the fish with a little of *prosciutto crudo* and a bit of butter and place them in a bowl.

Make a marinade with wine, olive oil, lemon juice, garlic and a pinch of salt and pepper and pour over the fish. Leave it for a couple of hours, turning the fish over a few times.

Preheat the oven to 355°F/180°C. Coat the red fish in the breadcrumbs and arrange them in one layer in an oiled ovenproof dish. Cook for approximately 15 minutes, or until the fish is cooked, sprinkle with 2 teaspoons of the marinade from time to time, to prevent the fish from drying out.

Serve straight from the dish.

Scampi in crosta di fritti serviti con patate e funghi sopra letto di spinaci

DEEP-FRIED SCAMPI OVER FRIED POTATOES, MUSHROOMS AND SPINACH

Fresh scampi and vegetables of the earth make this dish both healthy and tasty.

20 SCAMPI
¾ OZ/25 G MUSTARD
4¼ OZ/120 G BREADCRUMBS
¾ OZ/25 G CORNMEAL
2 LARGE POTATOES
3½ OZ/100 G MUSHROOMS
7 OZ/200 G FRESH SPINACH
1 ONION
1 CLOVE OF GARLIC
15 FL OZ/445 ML OLIVE OIL

Seasoning
SALT AND PEPPER

Cooking time: 30 minutes
Preparation time: 45 minutes
Serves: 4 people

Wash and peel the potatoes. Clean and chop the onion and mushrooms. Cut the potatoes into slices of no more than 3 mm thick. Put the vegetables together and season. Heat some oil in a frying pan and add the vegetables. After stirring the vegetables around, reduce the heat and cook for 25 minutes or until cooked. Keep turning the potatoes over in the pan to ensure they are cooked evenly.

While the potatoes are cooking clean the scampi and remove the shells. Using a brush, coat each of the scampi in the mustard. Put the cornmeal, breadcrumbs, salt and pepper in a bowl and roll the scampi in the mixture. Leave to the side. Start to heat the oil in preparation for the scampi. Wash the spinach and dry. Add some oil to a frying pan. When the oil is hot add the chopped garlic and spinach and cook for a few minutes and season. Place the potatoes in the centre of each plate and cover them in the spinach. Deep-fry the scampi for no more than 2 minutes and place on the top of the potatoes and spinach.

Palombo con i piselli

MONKFISH/HUSS AND FRESH PEA CASSEROLE

Monkfish is found on many of the menus in today's restaurants. The reason for this is the meat is very tasty and tender. Did you know that monkfish is from the same family as is shark? Well, don't let that put you off or you will be missing out on this great recipe.

1 LB 8½ OZ/750 G HUSS OR MONKFISH
1 FL OZ/30 ML OLIVE OIL
3 CLOVES GARLIC, PEELED AND FINELY CHOPPED
1 HANDFUL PARSLEY, FINELY CHOPPED
1 LB 8½ OZ/750 G FRESH PEAS (SHELLED WEIGHT)
1 TOMATO
7 FL OZ/210 ML *PASSATA DI POMMODORO*
1 TSP/5 G TOMATO PASTE
SALT AND PEPPER

Preparation time: 20 minutes
Cooking time: 30 minutes
Serves 4 people

Trim the fish and cut it into steaks or chunks depending on its width. A larger, older fish will slice into thick steaks, whereas a smaller, younger fish must be cut into chunks. Rinse the fish, pat it dry and set it aside.

In a shallow saucepan wide enough for the fish, place the olive oil, garlic and parsley. *Sauté* for about 6 minutes, then add the peas and stir. Cook for about 3–4 minutes, add the *passata* and tomato *purée*, stir very carefully and cover. Simmer very slowly for about 10 minutes. Make sure that the peas are completely tender, especially if you are using fresh ones, and then arrange the fish in the saucepan in one layer with the peas and tomato. Season generously with salt and pepper, cover and simmer for approximately 5 minutes. Turn the fish over and simmer for another 5 minutes. Turn the fish once again and simmer for another 5–7 minutes.

Place the fish on a warm serving dish and cover with the peas and tomato. Serve at once.

Scampi in salsa di vino bianco con peperoncino

WHOLE SCAMPI IN WHITE WINE AND CHILLI

Scampi or shrimps are a great favorite in Tuscany, and each area along the coast perfumes its shrimp with different herbs and spices. This dish looks spectacular if prepared with whole scampi; however, these may be hard to find. Try using large shrimp in exactly the same way for an equally delicious result.

16 LARGE SCAMPI
FLOUR FOR DUSTING
1 TBSP/½ FL OZ/15 ML OLIVE OIL
1 CHILLI PEPPER, CHOPPED
1 GARLIC CLOVE, FINELY CHOPPED
6 TBSP/3 FL OZ/90 ML DRY WHITE WINE
4 TBSP/2 FL OZ/60 ML COGNAC
8 TBSP/4 FL OZ/120 ML FISH STOCK
2 SPRIGS OF PARSLEY
SALT AND PEPPER

Preparation time: 15 minutes
Cooking time: 10 minutes
Serves 4 people

Carefully remove the shell from the center of the scampi, keeping the scampi whole and leaving the head and tail.

Cover the scampi in flour and lightly *sauté* in a pan with olive oil, chopped chilli pepper, finely chopped garlic and a little salt. Cook for a couple of minutes until the scampi turn a reddish color, and then cover with the white wine. Allow this to evaporate for 2 minutes and then add the chopped parsley and *Cognac*. Add the fish stock and cook for another 5 minutes.

Serve hot on a plate and sprinkle with freshly ground black pepper and freshly chopped parsley.

Salsas

SAUCES

Italian sauces, especially for pasta, are important to all Italian recipes. They are simple, flavorful and delicious. What would great pasta be without a fresh pesto or creamy *carbonara* to engulf the taste buds? The two basic white Italian sauces are *balsamella* whose base is a combination of flour and fat with hot milk, and *salsa bianca,* where stock takes the place of the hot milk – used for *carbonara*. The most famous Italian sauce is the basic tomato sauce, which becomes a *ragù* when meat and/or mushrooms are added. One of the most flavorful Italian sauces is basil pesto – fresh basil, fresh parsley, fresh garlic, pine nuts, Parmesan, cheese and fresh olive oil.

The following four recipes are the most common and classic Italian sauces and all follow the fundamental rule of Italian cuisine – simplicity. *Carbonara's* origins are from Rome. Pesto's roots are from the North – specifically Genoa. Bolognese originates from Bologna and a classic tomato sauce is common all over Italy. The following four recipes have been mastered over centuries and are still the most common and well-loved sauces. Unlike many French sauces, which can break, Italian sauces, when using the philosophy of *quanto basto* – "the right amount", will always be appetizing and delectable.

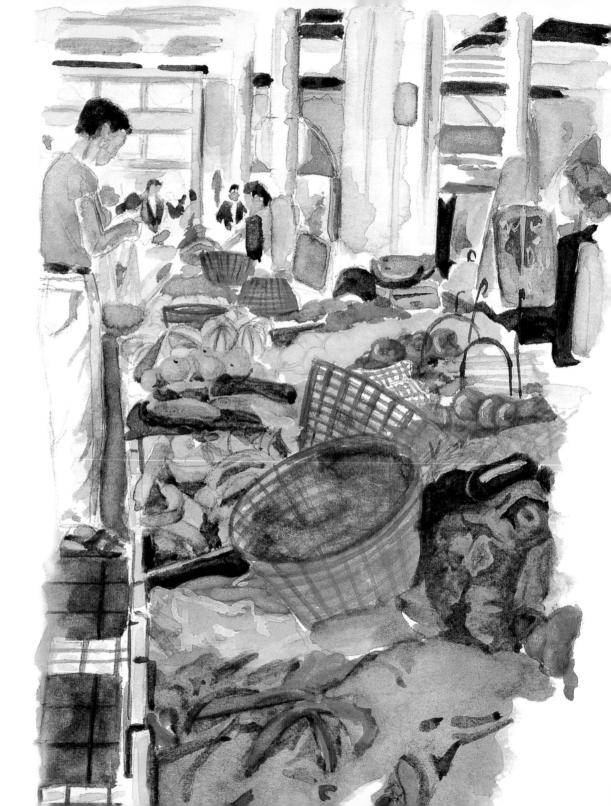

Sugo di pomodoro

FRESH TOMATO SAUCE

This is the most popular sauce in Italy because of the fragrance and taste. This sauce can be added to any kind of pasta. For a quick and tasty meal, add fresh basil and a touch of olive oil. The flavor of this sauce is classically Mediterranean.

1 LB 2 OZ/500 G FRESH TOMATOES OR CANNED TOMATOES
1 ONION
¼ CUP/55 G FRESH BASIL LEAVES
2 TBSP/1 FL OZ/30 ML OLIVE OIL
2 GARLIC CLOVES
SALT AND PEPPER

Preparation time: 10 minutes
Cooking time: 45 minutes
Serves 4 people

Heat the oil and *sauté* the chopped onion and garlic until they are soft and transparent. Add the salt, pepper, tomatoes and basil leaves. Simmer over a low heat as long as possible, adding a little water from time to time.

Chef's tip
You can change the style and taste of this sauce by simply adding different fresh herbs, garlic and different varieties of tomatoes.

Bolognese sauce

MEAT SAUCE

Outside Bologna, and especially outside Italy, the term designates a substantial meat sauce for pasta, known in Bologna simply as *ragù*. It is served on *tagliatelle*, not spaghetti, except on tourist menus.

1 LARGE ONION
1 STALK CELERY
2 CARROTS
1 OZ/30 G BUTTER
1 LB/450 G GROUND BEEF
4 TBSP/2 FL OZ/60 ML DRY RED WINE
1 CAN/14 OZ/400 G TOMATOES, SKINNED AND CHOPPED
1 TBSP/½ OZ/15 G TOMATO PASTE
1 TBSP/½ FL OZ/15 ML OLIVE OIL
2 PINCHES OF SALT
1 PINCH OF GROUND BLACK PEPPER
1¾ PT/1 LITER CHICKEN STOCK
PINCH OF SAGE
1 SPRIG OF ROSEMARY
1 BAY LEAF

Preparation time: 20 minutes
Cooking time: 45 minutes
Serves 4 people

Heat the oil in a frying pan and cook the meat. Use a fork to separate the meat. Strain the meat through a sieve to get rid of the fat. Chop the carrot and celery into a *brunoise*. In a large pot, melt the butter and add the vegetables, bay leaf, sage and rosemary. Stir occasionally for 5 minutes and add the meat. *Sauté* together for 2 minutes, and then add the red wine. Stir on a high heat for another 5 minutes and add the skinned and chopped tomatoes along with the tomato paste. Add the broth and cook for 1 hour 15 minutes on a medium heat. Stirring occasionally.

Chef's tip
Before adding the red wine, you can sprinkle the ingredients with a touch of white flour to make the sauce thicker. You can add butter (1¾ oz/50 g) after the sauce is cooked to add flavor.

Carbonara

CARBONARA SAUCE

The most popular white sauce in Italy, particularly in Rome where the sauce originated.

Preparation time: 20 minutes
Cooking time: 3 minutes
Serves 4 people

4 EGGS
1¾ OZ/50 G PARMESAN CHEESE
5¼ OZ/150 G *PANCETTA*/BACON
3½ OZ/10 G BUTTER
1½ TBSP/½ FL OZ/20 ML OLIVE OIL
3 TBSP/1¾ FL OZ/50 ML WHIPPING CREAM
SALT
WHITE PEPPER

Heat the oil and butter and fry the bacon for around 3 minutes. Beat the eggs, cheese and whipping cream together to create the sauce mixture, season with the salt and white pepper. Pour the mixture over the cooked pasta and stir continuously for 2–3 minutes, take the pasta off the heat and keep stirring. The heat from the cooked pasta will make sure that the eggs in the mixture are cooked thoroughly. Don't overcook the eggs otherwise you will end up with pasta and scambled eggs, just keep stirring until the mixture hardens into a sauce.

Chef's tip
This sauce is commonly served with cream as well, and is to be added at the same time as the eggs and cheese.

Pesto

PESTO SAUCE

Though the word pesto technically refers simply to any combination of herbs ground with a mortar and pestle, this basil sauce is the one we all know and love. The Ligurians are famous for their pesto (though its origins are actually Persian), and the sauce is used throughout the country.

Be careful when working with the basil – an old Tuscan superstition maintains that cutting it with a knife attracts snakes.

2 CUPS OF LOOSELY PACKED FRESH BASIL LEAVES
6 TBSP/3 FL OZ/90 ML OLIVE OIL
4 GARLIC CLOVES
2 TBSP/28 G PINE NUTS, TOASTED
1 TSP/5 G SEA SALT
½ CUP FRESHLY GRATED PARMESAN CHEESE

Preparation time: 15 minutes
Makes one cup of pesto

Put the basil leaves, garlic, pine nuts and the salt into a food processor and blend together. Slowly add the olive oil a little at a time.

The grated Parmesan should be added only after all the ingredients are blended well together.

Chef's tip
Be sure not to season the pesto too heavily with salt as Parmesan is a well-cured cheese and already gives a strong salty taste to the pesto.

Contorni

SIDE DISHES

On Italian menus, vegetables are often listed as *contorni*. The literal meaning is "contours" or "shapes", but the closest English equivalent is probably "side dishes". *Contorni* are served as accompaniments to the main course, but that description does not give them their due.

Vegetables have long been the glory of Italian cuisine, and in Tuscany, they are especially important. As they come in season, many restaurants create special menus with a vegetable in multiple courses. As *contorni*, no more than two vegetables will be served as accompaniments, and they will typically be prepared in a very simple manner. *Contorni* can be served with the main course, or after, on their own plates.

Carciofi in piede alla Fiorentina

FLORENTINE-STYLE ARTICHOKES

The best artichokes in Tuscany are the small purple ones that come from the area around Grosseto, a southern city near the sea. But the variety is endless: big ones, little ones, violet ones; served boiled, steamed, even raw with lemon juice. This recipe is based on a classic Florentine recipe where artichokes are filled with a savory mixture of *pancetta* and parsley, drizzled with olive oil, and braised.

8 MEDIUM ARTICHOKES
JUICE OF ½ A LEMON
3½ OZ/100 G *PANCETTA* OR BACON, CHOPPED
1 TBSP/14 G CHOPPED FRESH PARSLEY
SALT AND PEPPER
6 TBSP/3 FL OZ/90 ML OLIVE OIL
6 TBSP/3 FL OZ/90 ML WATER

Preparation time: 55 minutes
Cooking time: 30 minutes
Serves 4 people

Remove and discard the entire hard exterior leaves and the spiky tips of the artichokes. You should end up with a stalk, heart and three-quarters of the tender leaves. Peel the stalks until you get to the tender part and soak them in cold water, to which you have added lemon juice. Leave the artichokes to soak for 30 minutes.

Drain the artichokes thoroughly and place them so they fit tightly into a flameproof casserole or heavy saucepan, with the tips upwards.

Sprinkle the artichokes with chopped *pancetta* or bacon and parsley, season generously with salt and pepper and add oil and water in equal parts. There should be enough liquid to keep the artichokes moist but not immersed, about a quarter full.

Cover and simmer slowly for 25 minutes, adding a little more water should the bottom of the saucepan become dry. Now and again, gather the gravy with a spoon and pour it over the artichokes for added flavor.

Fagiolini con pancetta

GREEN BEANS AND PANCETTA

This vegetable and bacon dish can be served on the plate of any main course. It makes a great change from boiled vegetables.

1 LB 2 OZ/500 G OF GREEN BEANS
5¼ OZ/155 G *PANCETTA* OR BACON, SLICED
2 TBSP/1 FL OZ/30 ML BUTTER, MELTED
2 TBSP/1 FL OZ/30 ML OLIVE OIL
1 GARLIC CLOVE
SALT AND GROUND BLACK PEPPER TO SEASON

Preparation time: 15 minutes
Cooking time: 5–10 minutes
Serves 4 people

Clean the beans (top and tail) and boil until *al dente*. Drain the beans once cooked and divide them into bunches of six. Wrap the bacon around the individual bunches of beans. Put these in a tray and cover with melted butter, olive oil, and crushed garlic. Bake in a medium oven (355°F/180°C) for 5–10 minutes or until the bacon is cooked.

Parmigiana di melanzane

BAKED EGGPLANTS WITH CHEESE

Eggplants have a wonderful flavor and due to their sponge-like characteristics they absorb flavors easily. This dish is perfect as an accompaniment to a meat dish or can be served on its own as a vegetarian main course.

3 LB 5 OZ/1½ KG EGGPLANTS
SALT
8 TBSP/4 FL OZ/120 ML OLIVE OIL
1 ONION
4½ LB/2 KG TOMATOES
3 FRESH BASIL LEAVES
2 TSP/10 G DRIED BASIL
SALT AND FRESHLY GROUND BLACK PEPPER TO SEASON
FLOUR FOR DUSTING
5½ OZ/150 G GRATED PARMESAN CHEESE
8¾ OZ/250 G MOZZARELLA CHEESE, THINLY SLICED

Preparation time: 40–50 minutes
Cooking time: 30 minutes
Serves 4 people

Trim the stems. Slice the eggplants and into rounds. Sprinkle each slice with a little salt and place the salted slices in a colander. Cover with a plate and weight it down. Leave the eggplants to drain for approximately 30 minutes.

To make the tomato sauce: heat 4 tablespoons of the olive oil in a heavy pan, and *sauté* the onion until soft and golden. Add the chopped tomatoes and basil leaves, mix well and simmer gently, uncovered, until the mixture reduces to a thick sauce. Season to taste with salt and pepper.

Rinse the eggplant slices thoroughly in cold water to remove the saltiness. Pat dry with paper towels and dust with flour. Heat a little of the remaining olive oil in a large frying pan and *sauté* the eggplant in batches, adding more oil as needed, until they are cooked and golden brown on both sides. Drain on paper towels. Oil an ovenproof dish and arrange a layer of eggplant slices in the bottom of the dish. Sprinkle with Parmesan cheese and cover with mozzarella cheese slices. Spoon some of the tomato sauce over the top and continue layering up in this way until all the ingredients are used up, ending with a layer of tomato sauce and Parmesan cheese. Bake in a preheated oven at 390°F/200°C for 30 minutes.

Chef's tip
*Serve hot,
warm or cold.*

Patate arrostite con rosmarino

ROSEMARY ROASTED POTATOES

Although potatoes are popular in northern Italy, they are not always eaten on a daily basis. This recipe for potatoes which are crisp and golden on the outside and soft in the center, are baked in the oven rather than on the stovetop and grill, unlike most other typically Tuscan recipes in this book.

2¼ LB/1 KG PEELED POTATOES
2 WHOLE GARLIC CLOVES
2 SPRIGS FRESH ROSEMARY
7 FL OZ/210 ML OLIVE OIL
COARSE SEA SALT
GROUND BLACK PEPPER TO TASTE

Preparation time: 10 minutes
Cooking time: 50 minutes
Serves 4 people

Peel the potatoes and cut into large cubes of approximately the same size, ideally 1 in./2.5 cm squares. Heat the olive oil and garlic in a large pan over a stovetop. Once the oil is very hot, add the potatoes, rosemary, salt and stir well. Allow the potatoes to roast over the heat for 10 minutes, making sure they are well coated in the oil.

Transfer the pan to a preheated oven at 355°F/180°C and continue to cook until golden, approximately 30–40 minutes. The potatoes should be turned only once, and very carefully, when they are in the oven – if you turn them too much, they will start to break into little pieces. Once cooked, drain immediately so the potatoes do not continue to soak up the oil. Season with salt and pepper and serve immediately.

Peperoni e melanzane ripieni

STUFFED PEPPERS AND EGGPLANTS

Eggplants or aubergines as they are also known, are ideal for stuffing with ample portions and flesh that easily absorbs other flavors. Like eggplants, peppers are also ideal for stuffing; once the seeds have been removed, their hollow insides can easily be packed full.

2 EGGPLANTS
1 LARGE YELLOW BELL PEPPER
1 LARGE RED BELL PEPPER
6 TBSP/3 FL OZ/90 ML OLIVE OIL
2 TOMATOES
2 OZ/55 G CANNED ANCHOVY FILLETS
2 GARLIC CLOVES
2 TBSP/1 OZ/30 G CHOPPED FRESH BASIL OR MARJORAM
2 TBSP/1 OZ/30 G CHOPPED FRESH PARSLEY
2¾ OZ/80 G GRATED PECORINO OR PARMESAN CHEESE
2 TBSP/1 OZ/30 G PINE NUTS
2 OZ/55 G FRESH WHITE BREADCRUMBS
SALT AND PEPPER TO SEASON

Preparation time: 15 minutes
Cooking time: 50 minutes
Serves 4 people

Cut the eggplants and peppers in half lengthways. Carefully scoop out the eggplant flesh, chop it roughly and *sauté* in 2 tablespoons of the olive oil until golden and soft.

Remove the seeds and stalks from the peppers. Peel and seed the tomatoes. In a bowl, mix together the chopped tomatoes, anchovies, finely chopped garlic, basil or marjoram and parsley. Add 2 oz/55 g of the grated cheese, pine nuts, breadcrumbs and the *sautéed* eggplant mixture. Season to taste with salt and pepper.

Fill the hollow eggplants and peppers with the breadcrumb mixture, smoothing the surface of each. Arrange the stuffed eggplants and peppers on a large, oiled, shallow ovenproof dish. Sprinkle the remaining grated cheese and drizzle the remaining olive oil over the top. Bake in a preheated oven at 390°F/200°C for 50 minutes or until golden brown.

Chef's tip
The stuffed eggplants and peppers can be served hot or cold.

Capponaia di verdure fresche di stagione

RATATOUILLE OF FRESH VEGETABLES

This vegetable dish originates from Sicily, in fact it is known as *Capponata alla Siciliana*. This dish can accompany meat, fish or pasta dishes. The combination of these vegetables being cooked together creates the most fantastic aromas ... how you would imagine Mediterranean cuisine to be.

1 ONION
1 ZUCCHINI
1 SMALL YELLOW PEPPER
1 SMALL RED PEPPER
1 EGGPLANT
5 TBSP/2½ FL OZ/75 ML OLIVE OIL
1 GARLIC CLOVE
4 TBSP/2 FL OZ/60 ML TOMATO SAUCE
1 PINCH CHOPPED BASIL

Preparation time: 20 minutes
Cooking time: 15 minutes
Serves 4 people

Rinse and dry the zucchini, the peppers, and the eggplant. Chop the onion, peppers, and zucchini into ¾ in./2 cm cubes then cut the eggplant into 1½ in./4 cm cubes.

Heat the oil in a pan, add the onion along with the crushed garlic clove; *sauté* until golden brown, and remove the garlic. Add the eggplant and cook for 2 minutes, then cook the peppers for 5 minutes. At this time, add the zucchini and cook for another 5 minutes. Add the tomato sauce and cook for 3 minutes. Season and drizzle in some olive oil to give a nice, shiny finish. Add the chopped basil and serve.

Chef's tip
Try adding capers and pine nuts with the basil, at the end.

Verdura alla griglia

GRILLED VEGETABLES

Nearly every Italian household has a large, cast-iron grill to be used on the stove. If you do not have such a grill, a cast-iron frying pan can be used instead, but you will probably need to cook in smaller batches. The secret is to make sure that the heat is not too fierce or the vegetables will burn. No oil is used on the grill; otherwise, the vegetables become very limp and greasy. It is best to season the vegetables once they have been cooked.

1 ZUCCHINI
1 CARROT
1 LEEK
1 FENNEL BULB
1 EGGPLANT
1 ARTICHOKE, CUT IN HALF WITH THISTLE REMOVED
1 TOMATO
1 MEDIUM-SIZED CELERY ROOT
EXTRA-VIRGIN OLIVE OIL
COARSE SEA SALT
FINELY CHOPPED PARSLEY

Preparation time: 20 minutes
Cooking time: 20 minutes
Serves 6 people

Cut the vegetables into very fine slices with a sharp knife or if possible use a mandolin. The vegetables used should be no more than ⅓ in./7 mm thick (excluding the tomatoes, which should be about ½ in./1.5 cm thick).

Once all the vegetables are cut, dry grill them without any oil or seasoning. Arrange the grilled vegetables on a plate and dress with olive oil, salt, and a sprinkling of chopped parsley.

Chef's tip
These vegetables are perfect for cooking on the barbeque grill, which also simplifies the eventual clean up.

Polenta

CORN MEAL

Like pasta in the South, *polenta* has become a staple for northern Italians. As with pasta, it is very versatile, adapting easily to many different flavors. It can be served like pasta, topped with tomato sauce, but it is best as an accompaniment, its mild flavor being a good partner for spicy foods like stews and sauces.

There are two types of *polenta,* white and yellow. White *polenta* is made around Venice and uses only the inside of the corn, not the husk. It is considered to be more luxurious than yellow *polenta*, which is associated more with peasant cooking, although it can be equally tasty if prepared well. There are also degrees of coarseness: fine-ground is usually considered the best, although coarse-ground can often add extra texture to a dish.

2½ PT/1½ LITERS WATER
9 OZ/270 G COARSE CORN MEAL
1 TSP/5 G SALT

Preparation time: 10 minutes
Cooking time: 40 minutes
Serves 4 people

In a large pan bring the water to a boil. Add the salt and corn meal, whisking continuously to ensure no lumps develop. Continue to cook over a low heat for approximately 40 minutes, stirring occasionally with a wooden spoon. The *polenta* is finished when it pulls away from the side of the pan.

Pour the *polenta* on to a platter and serve immediately. Or, as an alternative, pour the *polenta* onto a damp tray or board and spread flat to about ½ in./1.5 cm thick with a damp rolling pin. Leave to cool in the refrigerator until set and then cut it into squares or rounds.

The *polenta* can then be prepared in several ways; deep-fried in olive oil and served as *crostini*. As a less oily alternative, try brushing each piece on both sides with olive oil and grill the *polenta* (both sides) and serve with meat or fish as an accompaniment.

Chef's tip
Traditional polenta *is cut with a thread instead of a knife.*

Dolci

DESSERTS

There are not many real Tuscan desserts, but those that do exist are nearly always linked to some form of religious celebration, e.g. Carnival, Easter, and Christmas. They include sweet flat breads and cakes, rice and semolina puddings and biscuits. Since the Middle Ages, Tuscans have flavored many of their cakes with aniseed (such as the *bucellato*, Lucca's most famous cake) as it not only gave flavor but was also thought to ward off evil spells. Innumerable Tuscan cakes are also made with chestnuts and chestnut flour – *castagnaccio* being the most traditional.

In Lucchesia, roasted chestnuts sprinkled with *grappa* often end an autumn dinner. One of the most well known of Tuscan biscuits is *cantucci*, which are made with almonds and are so hard that they are always dipped in a glass of *Vin Santo* before being eaten.

Biscotti (or cantucci)

TWICED BAKED ALMOND BISCUITS

These famous biscuits from Prato, a town near Florence, are closely associated with the sweet dessert wine, *Vin Santo*. The sophisticated almond-shaped biscuits are usually accompanied by a glass of *Vin Santo* and are often served for dessert or after-dinner accompaniment.

5¼ OZ/150 G SWEET WHOLE ALMONDS
8¾ OZ/250 G PLAIN WHITE FLOUR
8¾ OZ/250 G SUGAR
2 EGGS
SALT, PINCH
EXTRA FLOUR FOR DUSTING

Preparation time: 10–15 minutes
Cooking time: 35 minutes
Makes approximately 25 biscuits

Toast the almonds in the oven for several minutes, until lightly browned. Once toasted, chop them roughly. Sift the flour into a large bowl; add the sugar, salt and almonds. Blend in the eggs and knead or mix until soft elastic dough is formed. Roll the dough into small loaves. Place the loaves onto an oiled and floured baking tray. Bake for approximately 25 minutes, at 355°F/180°C or until they are a light golden brown. Remove the loaves from the oven and slice individual biscuit pieces approximately ½ in./1.5 cm thick and return to bake until a deep golden brown, which should take an additional 10 minutes.

Serve with traditional *Vin Santo* or as an alternative, sweet, medium or dry dessert wine. These biscuits are also great served with coffee.

Chef's tip
Although the almond biscotti/cantucci is the classic Italian version, try experimenting with different flavors. Interesting variations include chocolate and pistachio or chocolate and crystallized ginger.

Budino di pesche

PEACH PUDDING

This delicious way of serving peaches is especially good with older, end-of-season peaches. You can also make the dish with fruits such as apricots, large plums or nectarines.

10 RIPE PEACHES
8 FL OZ/240 ML DRY WHITE WINE
3 TBSP/42 G GRANULATED SUGAR
3 EGG WHITES, CHILLED
1 TBSP/14 G UNSALTED BUTTER

Preparation time: 1 hour
Cooking time: 55 minutes
Serves 4 people

Put the peaches into a saucepan with the wine and sugar. Poach slowly until the peaches are soft enough to sieve. Remove from the heat and push the peaches through a sieve to get a pulp.

Return the peach pulp to the heat, and allow it to boil gently to remove excess moisture. When the pulp is thick (like jam) remove from the heat and set aside to cool.

Whisk the chilled egg whites until completely stiff. Fold them into the peach mixture. Butter a 1¾ pt/1 liter smooth-sided mold and pour in the mixture. Place the mold in a *bain-marie* for approximately 45 minutes, never allowing the water to come to a boil. As soon as the pudding is well set, take it off the heat; leave to cool, and then put it in a bowl to serve.

Zabaglione

WHIPPED WINE CUSTARD

On menus, you may also see this dish spelled *zabaione* or *zabajone*. Italians consider *zabaglione* to be the ultimate refinement of custard: light and airy, yet rich. Tuscans sometimes substitute *Vin Santo* for *Marsala*, though more may be required because of the lower alcohol content.

4 EGG YOLKS
5 TBSP SUGAR
8 TBSP/4 FL OZ/120 ML *MARSALA* OR SWEET WHITE WINE

Preparation time: 20 minutes
Cooking time: 15 minutes
Serves 4–6 people

Separate the eggs. In a bowl, whisk the egg yolks then transfer them into the top of a double boiler, or in a basin sitting over a small saucepan of gently simmering water. Make sure the basin is not in contact with the water below. Add the sugar and *Marsala*, or sweet white wine, to the egg yolks and stir well.

Beat the mixture with either a wire whisk or a hand-held electric mixer until the *zabaglione* is thick, light and hot. If you are using a wire whisk, this will take 10–15 minutes, so be patient. Check that the water simmers gently underneath and does not boil dry. When the *zabaglione* is cooked, pour it carefully into four small glasses and serve immediately.

To serve it cold, continue beating the mixture, off the heat, until it has cooled completely. Mix the cold *zabaglione* with raspberries or sliced strawberries or peaches.

Soufflé di Amaretto

AMARETTO ALMOND SOUFFLÉS

Soufflés are not commonly prepared in Italy and are more French in origin. This recipe combines the wonderful taste of the well-known Italian Amaretto liqueur with the light and airy texture of *soufflé*.

Base
4 MACAROONS
5 TBSP/2½ FL OZ/75 ML AMARETTO DI SARONNO

Almond *purée*
2¾ OZ/75 G FLAKED ALMONDS
10 TBSP/5 FL OZ/150 ML MILK
2 TSP/10 G SUGAR

Soufflé
10 TBSP/5 FL OZ/150 ML MILK
1 DROP VANILLA EXTRACT
½ OZ/15 G BUTTER
1 OZ/30 G WHITE FLOUR
4 EGG YOLKS (1 KEPT SEPARATELY)
4 EGG WHITES
1 OZ/30 G SUGAR
SIFTED CONFECTIONERS' SUGAR TO DECORATE

Preparation time: 20 minutes
Cooking time: 10–12 minutes
Serves 4 people

Grease and flour four 3 in./7.5 cm individual *soufflé* dishes. Soak the macaroons in half of the Amaretto and put one macaroon, cut into quarters, in each prepared *soufflé* dish.

Put the almonds, milk and sugar into a saucepan and bring to a boil. Reduce the heat and simmer gently for several minutes. Cool slightly and then blend in a food processor until thoroughly mixed.

For the *soufflé*, put two-thirds of the milk (3¼ fl oz/100 ml) in a heavy saucepan with the vanilla and butter and bring to a boil. Remove from the heat and stir in the remaining milk with the flour and one egg yolk. Heat again until the mixture thickens and whisk briefly. Add the remaining egg yolks and cook for 2 minutes over a low heat. Beat the egg whites until stiff and whisk in the sugar. Blend the *soufflé* mixture with the almond *purée* and remaining Amaretto. Carefully fold in the beaten egg whites.

Spoon this mixture into the *soufflé* dishes and cook in a preheated oven at 430°F/220°C for 10–12 minutes. Dust with the confectioners' sugar.

Torta di pera e fichi

PEAR AND FIG TART

Tarts are a favorite Tuscan dessert, and in fact are so beloved that they are often eaten for breakfast and as snacks throughout the day. The combination of figs and pears in this tart produces great texture and flavor. Use the basis of this recipe with other seasonal fruits to create your own delicious tarts.

7 OZ/200 G PUFF PASTRY (PRE-PREPARED PASTRY)
1¾ OZ/50 G FLOUR
4 PEARS
4 FIGS
10 TBSP/5 FL OZ/150 ML HONEY
5¼ OZ/150 G BUTTER
1 TSP/5 G CINNAMON

Preparation time: 10 minutes
Cooking time: 15 minutes
Serves 4 people

Dust a board with the flour and roll out the pastry. Make 4–6 circles of 6 in./15 cm in diameter.

Peel and core the pears, slice into thin lengthwise slices. Wash and cut the figs into thin, lengthwise slices. Place alternating pear and fig slices in a fan shape around the pastry circles and sprinkle on the cinnamon. Melt the butter and honey in a pot and with a brush, brush the honey mixture over the fruit.

Bake in a preheated oven at 430°F/220°C for 5 minutes. Reduce the oven temperature to 390°F/200°C and bake for another 10 minutes.

Serve hot with vanilla ice cream or fresh cream.

Frittelle di castagne

CHESTNUT FLOUR FRITTERS

An abundance of chestnut trees in the hilly and mountainous areas of Tuscany meant that, for many centuries, chestnuts were part of the staple diet and, indeed for the poorer classes, provided an inexpensive form of nutrition. This very aromatic flour can be an acquired taste, but it is a taste very reminiscent of Tuscany. These lovely fritters make a great dessert on cold winter evenings, and the fruit and nuts make a lovely complement to the sweet taste of the chestnut flour.

10½ OZ/300 G CHESTNUT FLOUR
1 TBSP/½ OZ/15 G RAISINS
2 TBSP/1 OZ/30 G PINE NUTS
1 FRESH ROSEMARY SPRIG
SALT
WATER (ENOUGH TO MAKE A BATTER)
OLIVE OIL, FOR DEEP-FRYING
SUGAR, TO SERVE

Preparation time: 10 minutes
Cooking time: 30 minutes
Makes approximately 20 fritters

Mix the flour with the raisins, pine nuts, rosemary leaves and a pinch of salt and enough water to make a thick batter mixture.

Heat the oil in a frying pan (skillet) until very hot. Scoop spoonfuls of the mixture into the frying pan and fry until golden brown. Drain on a paper towel.

Serve very hot, sprinkled with sugar.

RHODE SCHOOL of CUISINE

Sorbetto al limone

LEMON SORBET

Sorbet differs from ice cream in that it is water rather than dairy based. Experiment with different fruit pulps to make your own delicious, individual variations.

8¾ OZ/250 G SUGAR
10 TBSP/5 FL OZ/150 ML WATER
½ OZ/15 G OF LEMON *ZESTE*
16¾ FL OZ/500 ML LEMON JUICE

Preparation time: 30 minutes
Refrigeration time: 2 hours
Serves 4 people

In a medium pot, mix together the sugar, water and lemon *zeste*. Gently heat the mixture until the sugar melts, then slowly bring to a boil. Add the lemon juice and place the mixture in an ice-cream machine until hard. Place in the freezer until ready to use.

Chef's tip
Sorbets are appropriate and delicious when served in between courses to clean the palate.

Torta della nonna

GRANDMA'S PIE

"*Torta della nonna* is a traditional Tuscan cake that is either dry and flat or made with a thick pastry crust filled with custard. This is my personal variation, which my grandmother used to make for me when I was a child. I still remember how good it was to this day."

Giancarlo Talerico

This sweet short crust pastry, made with eggs, flour, butter and sugar, is the most popular pastry base for tarts in Italy.

Sweet paste
1 LB 2 OZ/510 G FLOUR
10½ OZ/300 G BUTTER
7 OZ/200 G SUGAR
1 PINCH OF SALT
4 EGGS
ZESTE OF ½ A LEMON
1 TSP VANILLA EXTRACT

Filling
16¾ FL OZ/500 ML MILK
4 EGGS
3½ OZ/100 G SUGAR
2½ OZ/70 G FLOUR
2½ OZ/70 G PINE NUTS
VANILLA POD/BEAN

Preparation time: 2 hours + 3 hours for the sweet paste
Cooking time: 35 minutes
Serves 4 people

For the sweet paste, sieve the flour into a large bowl and make a well in the center. Add the butter, sugar, eggs, lemon *zeste* and vanilla extract into the well. Slowly start to mix, gradually bringing the flour to the center. Once combined, put the paste into the refrigerator to rest for 3 hours before using.

To make the filling, in a pot, boil the milk with the vanilla pod/bean (cut the bean in half to release the flavors). Beat, all in one bowl, three of the eggs with the sugar and flour. Add the previously boiled milk and stir to combine. Place everything back into the pot and bring to a boil.

Fill individual pie dishes (or one large dish) with sweet paste and leave to cool. Once the sweet paste has cooled, fill with two-thirds of the cream. Add half of the nuts; cover this with another layer of sweet paste. With the remaining egg, separate the yolk and whisk it in a small bowl to be used as an egg wash. With a pastry brush, brush over the cakes before adding the remaining nuts. Cook in a preheated oven at 390°F/200°C for 35 minutes.

Serve warm garnished with pine nuts and vanilla.

Chef's tip
To make the preparation of the sweet paste easier, try working the butter and sugar together before adding to the flour.

Vaniglia gelato

VANILLA ICE CREAM

Italians are justly famous for their *gelati*, perhaps the best ice cream in the world. The Chinese created sorbets, which the Arabs introduced to the Sicilians in the eleventh century, but the refined delicacy we know today goes back to the seventeenth century.

   Hints of other flavors, banana, lemon and prunes, are typically added to enhance the flavor of the main ingredient. Any number of liqueurs can be used to give the vanilla ice cream extra flavor. Once you know the basic recipe for ice cream, you can be creative and make everything from dark or white chocolate to toffee, raspberry, peach or anything you like.

16¾ FL OZ/500 ML FRESH MILK
5 EGG YOLKS
1 VANILLA POD/BEAN
5¼ OZ/150 G SUGAR
ZESTE FROM ½ A LEMON (AVOID ANY WHITE)
8½ FL OZ/250 ML OF WHIPPING CREAM

Preparation time: 1 hour
Serves 4 people

Beat the egg yolks and sugar together in a large bowl. In a pot, gently heat the milk and whipping cream with the vanilla and lemon *zeste*, bring to a boil and add the egg mix. Cook the mixture over a *bain-marie* until the temperature of the mixture reaches 185°F/85°C. Strain the mixture and place in the ice-cream machine until hard.

Tiramisu

SOAKED LADYFINGERS WITH MASCARPONE CHEESE AND COFFEE

Meaning, "pick me up", this is one of the most popular desserts throughout Italy, especially in wintertime. There are many ways to make *tiramisu*, some with a consistency similar to American cheesecake, and some very light and airy. This version is on the lighter side.

2 EGG YOLKS
2 TBSP SUGAR
A FEW DROPS OF VANILLA EXTRACT
8¾ OZ/250 G MASCARPONE CHEESE
12 TBSP/6 FL OZ/180 ML STRONG BLACK COFFEE
2 TBSP/1 FL OZ/30 ML *MARSALA*
5¼ OZ/150 G SPONGE/LADY FINGERS
1 TBSP/15 G UNSWEETENED COCOA POWDER
2 TBSP/30 G GRATED DARK CHOCOLATE

Preparation time: 20 minutes (3–4 hours' refrigeration time)
Serves 4 people

Mix the egg yolks and sugar together in a bowl until creamy. Add the vanilla and fold in the mascarpone cheese. The mixture should be thick and creamy.

Make the strong black coffee, and then mix with the *Marsala* in a bowl. Quickly dip the sponge fingers into the coffee mixture. They should absorb just enough liquid to add flavor. Do not allow the sponge fingers to go soggy and fall apart.

Arrange several of the soaked sponge fingers in the base of a large attractive glass serving bowl or four individual dessert glasses. Cover with a layer of the mascarpone mixture. Continue with alternating layers of sponge fingers and mascarpone, finishing with a top layer of mascarpone. Sift the cocoa over the top and sprinkle with grated chocolate. Chill in the refrigerator for 3–4 hours or until set.

Chef's tip
The flavor improves if the tiramisu *is left overnight. Also, in Tuscany,* Vin Santo *is used in place of* Marsala.

Rocciata d'Assisi

ASSISI PASTRY

These lovely, light biscuits are named after the "holy city" of Assisi, which lies to the east of Perugia. They are perfect to serve after dinner with *Vin Santo* or coffee.

8¾ OZ/250 G WHITE FLOUR (PLUS EXTRA FOR DUSTING)
9¾ OZ/280 G SUGAR
6 TBSP/3 FL OZ/90 ML SUNFLOWER OIL
SALT, PINCH
11 TBSP/5½ FL OZ/175 ML WATER
2 APPLES, CORED AND PEELED
1¾ OZ/50 G CURRANTS
2½ OZ/75 G RAISINS
3½ OZ/100 G WALNUTS
3½ OZ/100 G DRIED FIGS
3½ OZ/100 G HAZELNUTS
6 TBSP/3 FL OZ/90 ML *MARSALA*
3½ OZ/100 G BLANCHED ALMOND SLIVERS
4 TBSP/56 G CONFECTIONERS' SUGAR

Preparation time: 20 minutes
Cooking time: 40 minutes
Serves 4–6 people

In a large bowl, blend the flour with 1 tablespoon of sugar, 1½ tablespoons of oil and the salt. Add enough water to make smooth pliable dough. Roll the dough out on a floured work surface until it is as thin as possible without tearing.

Mix the peeled, cored and sliced apples, currants, raisins, dried figs, chopped walnuts, hazelnuts and blanched almond slivers together with the remaining sugar and blend in the *Marsala*. Use this mixture to fill the center of the pastry sheet. Roll the pastry up on itself to encase the fruit and nut mixture. Carefully seal the edges all round, then bend the filled pastry to make a horseshoe shape. Use half the remaining oil to grease a baking sheet. Lay the pastry on top and rub the remaining oil over the surface. Bake in a preheated oven at 355°F/180°C for approximately 40 minutes until crisp and golden brown. Leave to cool on a wire rack then dust with confectioners' sugar before serving.

M

Marsala
A rich dessert wine produced in the South of Italy and Sicily

Minestrone
A very thick vegetable soup sometimes with rice or pasta

Mirepoix
Carrots, onions and celery diced into cubes

Mortadella
The most popular of Italian sausages made from finely minced pork and coarsely diced pork fat

P

Pancetta
Italian bacon/salt cured pork belly, which can also be smoked

Passata di pommodoro
A *purée* of fresh, pasteurized tomato, in bottles/cans

Pecorino
A sheep's milk cheese. There are many different varieties – the best being made in Tuscany

Pinzimonio
Crudités of fresh, raw vegetables chopped into bite-size pieces and served with a dip such as vinaigrette or cidranette

Polenta
A sort of thick porridge made with corn flour that can be cooled, sliced, fried or grilled

Polpette
Meatballs made with minced meat, seasoned with herbs and cooked in a tomato sauce

Porcini
Wild mushrooms with broad, pale stalks and a thick, dark cap. The darker the cap, the better the mushroom. They are in season early autumn but can be found dried in slices (boletus).

Prosciutto crudo
A raw, salt-cured ham usually cut into very fine slices

R

Rapini
Also known as *rape* and *cime di rapa*. A turnip top with dark green leaves, sturdy stalks and clusters of small flowers. it is usually *sautéed* in oil with garlic or boiled and seasoned with olive oil and lemon

Ribollita
A hearty soup of vegetables and bread

Ricotta
In Tuscany this cheese is made from sheep's – or cows' – milk whey left after making pecorino cheese. The whey is reboiled and strained and left to thicken

Rucola
A type of salad leaf – *rocket*/arugula

S

Saltimbocca alla Romana
Slices of ham and veal seasoned with sage, fried in butter and then braised in white wine

Sfoglia
Any kind of dough that is flattened by a machine or rolling pin

T

Tagliare a filetti
To fillet – as in a piece of meat or a fish

Tartufo
Truffles, both black and white. These are highly aromatic and very costly fungi, which grow underground and are hunted with a dog or pig to sniff them out. The black truffle (finest are grown in Umbria) is less expensive but not as strong in taste as the white truffle *Topini*

U

All'uccelletto
"Like a bird" – describes dishes prepared with olive oil, garlic and sage – the classic mix for small game birds. A little tomato sauce is added to the Tuscan beans recipe *all'uccelletto*

V

Vin Santo
A Tuscan dessert wine traditionally served with *cantucci* (for dipping)

Z

Zabaglione
A dessert of egg yolk, sugar and *Marsala*

Pasta varieties

Bucatini	Hollow spaghetti used mainly in southern Italy
Cannelloni	Large filled pasta tubes of approximately 1 in./2.5 cm in diameter and 3 in./7.5 cm long. This type of pasta is usually filled with spinach and *ricotta*, baked in the oven and then topped with a sauce to complement, such as tomato and basil sauce
Capelli d'angelo or *capelvenere*	Angel's hair – a very thin pasta as long as spaghetti which is usually used in very fine sauces made with truffles, caviar, etc.
Conghiglie	Shell-shaped pasta generally used with a creamy type of sauce, which is held within the shape of the pasta
Ditalini	Very short macaroni of about 1 cm in length. Used with a vegetable pasta, especially beans
Farfalle	"Butterfly" pasta, also called bow ties
Fusilli	Small corkscrew-shaped tubes
Gemelli	Short pasta shapes of two strands "twins" which are twisted around each other
Gnocchi	Small dumplings made with flour and potatoes, which are turned against a fork to give them their characteristic ridges
Lasagne	Large, flat pasta traditionally layered and baked in the oven
Linguine	"Small tongues" of long, thin, flat strands
Macaroni/rigatoni	Big stripy tubes
Orrechiette	An ear-shaped pasta, ideal for a vegetable pasta such as broccoli or cauliflower
Pappardelle	One of the most Tuscan pastas which is very thinly rolled and cut into broad ribbons – it is usually served with rabbit or game sauce
Penne	"Quills" – tubes with angled ends, which resemble pen nibs
Ravioli	Two sheet of thin pasta with a filling in between
Reginette	a long, flat pasta similar to *tagliatelle* but with a wavy frilled edge
Rotelline	Wheel-shaped pasta
Spaghetti	The classic long, round strands with spaghetti being a slightly thinner version
Tagliatelle/fettuccine	A long, ribboned pasta
Taglierini/tagliolini	Usually a fresh pasta of the same length of spaghetti, but square instead of round
Tortelli/tordelli/ tortelloni	Fresh pasta traditionally stuffed with spinach and *ricotta* in Tuscany. The name varies according to the size, with *tortelli* being the smallest
Ziti	A hollow pasta – the larger version of *bucatini*

Herbs and spices

In the eyes of botanists, herbs are "plants with non-woody and non-persistent stems which die down to the ground after flowering". But for chefs and herbalists, herbs are more simply described as leafy parts of plants with culinary or medicinal uses, and spices are the non-leafy parts, such as seeds and bark, that bring aromatic or pungent flavors to the kitchen. Herbs and spices exist in vast array showing a spectacular diversity of form and flavor, and with a history of use by peoples around the world that is long and colorful. To glance at the herbal literature spanning centuries from the scholarly writings of ancient Greece and Rome, the early medical texts of China and India, and the mysterious medieval herbals of Europe, to the studies published today, is to capture a glimpse of the imaginative and fascinating world of the human use of plants.

One cannot help but wonder at the diversity of uses, be they medicinal, ritual, social, mythical or culinary, to which herbs, spices and many other plants have been put over the ages. We read of herbs like parsley (*Petroselinum crispum*) used to sweeten the breath, of meadowsweet (*Filipendula ulmaria*) and others used as strewing herbs to freshen the rooms of medieval Europe, of scented herbs like lavender and rose used in perfumes, of herbs as dyes such as indigo (*Indigofera tinctoria*) and woad (*Isatis tinctoria*), and many, many more. The list is as long as it is diverse, but

nowhere is our utilization and dependency on herbs greater or more valued than in food and medicine. As foods and flavorings, herbs and spices comprise an integral part of all cultures, their evolution influenced as much by climate, social and religious factors as it by history, politics and trade. A region's cuisine is a complex expression of its soul, its character, its history, and its relationship with the land. Seen in this context, a love of one's national cuisine is to be expected and celebrated.

The idea of food as medicine is an ancient one and there has been much written on the subject that is not discussed here. However, it is good to remember that fresh, aromatic herbs, so reminiscent of the scents of wild herbs crushed under foot on Mediterranean hillsides, can be good for the body, and impart fine and diverse flavors to food.

Anyone who has ever sown basil seeds in a sunny window box, waited for the first fresh leaves to unfold, nursed salad plants through the spring, harvested pungent chives for garnishing a simple summer supper, or cut fresh, aromatic sprigs of rosemary, knows that the joy of herbs lies not only in their culinary use but also with their cultivation and harvest. The advantages of fresh herbs cannot be underestimated, and the rewards of cooking with homegrown handfuls of aromatic leaves are well worth the efforts of growing them. You do not need to be an ambitious gardener, with a large garden, to start growing your own herbs. With seeds chosen from a reputable supplier and with care and attention, a pot in an urban kitchen or terracotta urns in a sunny yard can yield successful herb crops. Of course there will always be times, especially in winter, when you must rely on dried herbs. The difference in taste and pungency between fresh and dry herbs can be huge and this must be taken into account when cooking with them. For example, dried basil (*Ocimum basilicum*) is no substitute for the sweetly pungent taste of fresh, chopped basil leaves, though dried sage (*Salvia officinalis*), which retains its taste well on drying, makes a good substitute for the fresh leaves.

Being predominantly tropical in origin, spices are nearly always dried when we use them, and their names – cloves, cinnamon, star *anise*, nutmeg, mace – conjure up images of aromatic sacks in dusty warehouses, of ocean-trading ships, of colorful markets, and of the heady aromas of hot, far-off lands.

Strange as it might seem, the eating of flowers of certain species has a long history. From the consumption of the petals (but not the whole bitter flower) of pot marigolds in India and nasturtiums by the Persians, to the use of rose petals as flavorings in Europe, it can be seen that some flowers have had culinary as well as decorative uses. However, many flowers contain toxins and are poisonous, and therefore great care must be taken to ensure the safe consumption and correct identification of any flower before eating it. It is also important to note that the use of garden chemicals (e.g. growth sprays) could turn an edible flower into a poisonous one. As with all plants, it is wise to err on the side of caution, and if you are in any doubt about its toxicity then do not eat it! Only three species with edible flowers are given here, but the serious student of edible flowers is recommended Jekka McVicar's *Good Enough to Eat*, which describes the character and use of many other species.

The world of herbs and spices is a broad and colorful subject that is as fascinating to the mind as it is enticing to the palate and medicinal to the body. As a complement to the recipes of this book, a handful of these flavorings are described below, with an introduction to their characteristics, origins, and culinary use and cultivation. Each species is given with its common name but since these are easily confused, the scientific name, which acts as a unique tag, is also given. Limited by space, we can only include a short list of the more commonly used herbs and spices, but the reader must remember that there are many, many more species available which together offer an almost endless palate of tastes, textures, scents and colors. Discovery of this diversity of flavors is only the beginning. Restock your spice shelves, find your nearest source of fresh herbs (or plant some out in pots), add some imagination and time, and years of culinary experimentation and enjoyment will be yours.

Sasha Barrow

Sweet basil (*Ocimum basilicum*)

From the Greek *okimon*, meaning basil. Basil, a low-growing, annual herb, is generally thought to have an Indian origin, from where it reached Europe, via the Middle East, in the sixteenth century. There are many varieties of basil, all rich in the essential oils that impart the wonderfully, sweet aromatic flavor, so closely associated with the cuisine of the Mediterranean, particularly Italy. The fresh leaves are commonly added to rich, tomato-based dishes, to salads or are used as flavorsome garnishes for soups and stews. Basil is a crucial ingredient in the classical *soupe au pistou* of Provence and when mixed with pine nuts, garlic and Parmesan, forms the famous pesto sauce from Genoa in Italy. Basil has a sedative, calming affect and is used medicinally for nervous disorders, stress and headaches. Basil is easily grown from seed in light, warm and sunny conditions and its bushy growth can be encouraged by regular harvest of the upper leaves.

Parsley (*Petroselinum crispum*)

From the Greek *petros*, meaning rock and the Greek name *Selinum*.
Parsley is a short, stocky, biennial species of Mediterranean origin that is likely to have traveled west with the Romans. A common and well-known herb, parsley is widely used in European cuisine often as the basic ingredient in herb mixtures such as *bouquet garni*, or as flavoring in most savory dishes, or simply as a garnish. There are two main varieties of parsley: curly-leafed and the stronger-tasting flat-leafed parsley (French parsley). A long list of medicinal uses is recorded for parsley, ranging from its use as a diuretic to its regulatory effect on the digestive system. The herb is high in vitamin C, iron, magnesium and other minerals. Parsley can be easily grown from seed sown throughout spring and summer.

Tarragon (*Artemisia dracunculus*)

The botanical name is from the Greek goddess *Artemis*, and the common name *tarragon* is from the French *esdragon*, meaning "little dragon" or *dracunculus* in Latin.
A perennial herb, Eurasian in origin, tarragon is a low-growing herb with leaves that are commonly used in French cuisine. Their strong flavor enhances egg and chicken dishes particularly well, and adds a distinct flavor to vinegar (tarragon vinegar is essential for true tartar sauce), salad dressings, and sauces (such as *Béarnaise* sauce). Medicinally, tarragon is used as a general digestive aid, soothing flatulence, indigestion and nausea. Tarragon rarely flowers and therefore it is best grown from cuttings, planted in well-drained soil in warm, dry, sunny positions.

Chives (*Allium schoenoprasum*)

From the Latin *allium*, meaning garlic. A perennial plant of Eurasian origin, chives belong, with onions and garlic, to the genus *Allium* and share a similar, if less pungent, taste. Chopped chive leaves make an attractive and tasty garnish and go well with egg, cheese and some vegetable dishes. Chives sprinkled on buttered beetroot are a particularly good combination. The pretty purple flowers also have a mild onion flavor and can also be used, in moderation, as a garnish or in salads. Chives are rarely used medicinally, but are known to have antiseptic and antibiotic properties. Chives are easily cultivated from bulbs in moist, rich soils.

Chervil (*Anthriscus cerefolium*)

From the Greek name *Anthriskos*.
Native to southeastern Europe, chervil is a small, annual plant with a delicate flavor, somewhat similar to aniseed. It is commonly used in French cuisine, particularly in potato, egg, chicken and fish dishes. Chervil does not retain its flavor well when dried, and is best used fresh as a garnish, added to salads or, at the last moment, to cooked food. Chervil has diuretic properties and is used for circulatory problems. Chervil can be grown from seed sown in moist, semi-shaded conditions in early spring or late summer.

Garden thyme (*Thymus vulgaris*)

From the Greek name for thyme, *thymus*.
Thyme is a low-growing, woody herb, native to the Mediterranean and southern Europe, where its small and strongly, aromatic leaves have long been in culinary use. Unlike many herbs, thyme retains its flavor well on drying and is commonly used, fresh or dried, in herb mixes, such as *bouquet garni*, and in slow-cooked savory dishes, particularly those rich in onions, garlic and wine. Thyme's purple flowers are much loved by bees, and the resulting honey is highly valued. Thyme has astringent, antiseptic and anti-fungal properties and is used by herbalists to improve digestion and treat respiratory disorders. Thyme thrives in dry, well drained, gravelly soil, in sunny conditions.

Dill (*Anethum graveolens*)

From the Greek name for dill, *anethon*. An annual species with a fine, feathery appearance, dill is native to southern Europe, Russia, Iran and India. Valued as a culinary herb throughout its geographical range, it is particularly popular in Scandinavia where it is an important ingredient in pickles and vinegar and is typically added fresh, at the last moment, to fish, egg and potato dishes. In addition to its diuretic properties, dill has a calming and soothing effect on the digestive system. Dill can be grown from seed sown in spring in moist soil, and the leaves are best harvested before flowering.

Coriander, Cilantro (*Coriandrum sativum*)

From the Greek *koris*, meaning insect (apparently due to the similarity in smell between coriander leaves and that given off by some insects such as beetles).
An annual species, native to southern Europe, coriander has leaves and seeds with culinary and medicinal uses. Its wonderfully aromatic leaves are an essential herb for flavoring and garnishing many Asian and Middle Eastern dishes, and its ground seed is an important spice in curries and sweet baking. The medicinal properties of coriander relate mostly to the seeds rather than the leaves. Coriander can be grown from seed in fertile soil in warm, sunny conditions.

Rosemary (*Rosmarinus officinalis*)

From the Latin *ros*, meaning dew, and *marinus*, meaning sea. The name alludes to the blue flowers and coastal habitat of this species.

An evergreen, perennial species, native to the Mediterranean, rosemary is a woody, upright herb rich in aromatic essential oils. Its strong, resinous taste and tough texture are not to everyone's taste, but rosemary is much appreciated in southern Mediterranean cuisine where whole sprigs of the herb are used to enhance roast and salted meats and make wonderfully aromatic vinegar and dressings. Long since thought to improve memory and concentration, rosemary is also used to improve digestion and soothe headaches and nervous tension. Rosemary is cultivated easily from seeds or cuttings planted in light, well-drained soil in warm, sunny conditions.

Mint (*Mentha* species)

According to Greek myth, mint was created by the transformation of a nymph named *Menthe*.

There are many species of mint, and the ease with which they hybridize has led to a large number of cultivated varieties varying in appearance, culinary and medicinal qualities. Mints generally do not combine well with other herbs or with garlic and are best used alone. Spearmint (*Mentha viridis*) and peppermint (*M. × piperita*) are the species commonly used for mint tea, fruit salads, and in sauces and jellies eaten with meats, particularly lamb. Peppermint has a soothing effect on the digestive system and the leaves make a calming tea. Mint is best cultivated from cuttings planted in light, moist soil in sunny conditions.

Bay, Sweet laurel (*Laurus nobilis*)

From the Greek *laurus*. This herb has historically been a symbol of academic excellence and crowns of bay leaves were worn by the wise and victorious in ancient Greece and Rome.

A robust, woody, shrub or small tree, bay trees produce thick, glossy leaves that are used, fresh or dried, in savory soups, sauces and pickles. Bay also enhances sweet dishes; milk boiled with a bay leaf makes interesting custard. As an herb with bitter properties, bay improves appetite, soothes indigestion, colic and wind. Bay trees can be grown from cuttings in most soil types, in pots or gardens, in warm, sunny positions.

Common sage (*Salvia officinalis*)

From the Latin *salvere*, meaning to save or to heal.

An evergreen, low-growing species, native to the Mediterranean, sage has a long-held reputation as a "life prolonging" herb – sage tea was very popular in medieval England. Its culinary reputation developed somewhat later, and its strongly aromatic, slightly astringent leaves make good companions to robust dishes such as roast meats, sausages and stuffings. With astringent, antiseptic and anti-inflammatory properties, sage improves digestion and liver function. Sage is best cultivated from cuttings planted out in dry soil in sunny positions.

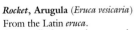

Rocket, **Arugula** (*Eruca vesicaria*)

From the Latin *eruca*.

As a small, sharp-tasting, annual species, native to the Mediterranean and Eastern Asia, rocket has been used as a salad vegetable since Roman times. The pungent and peppery leaves add a distinctive edge to summer salads and sandwiches. Various horticultural varieties exist, all of which are milder in flavor than the wild species. Rocket is easily grown from seed in rich, moist soil in sunny conditions. Rocket is primarily a culinary herb and is rarely used medicinally. The leaves should be harvested before flowering.

Spices

In Europe, the use of herbs has always been open to all, regardless of wealth, since many of the familiar herbs are wild-harvested or easily cultivated in home gardens. In contrast, spices are predominantly tropical in origin, and in the early days of the spice trade, only the wealthy could afford to buy these exotic flavorings. Fascinating in historical, political, cultural and social terms, the story of the global spice trade is peppered with anecdotes as pungent as the spices themselves, and there are many books on the subject.

Cinnamon (*Cinnamomum verum*)
From the Greek *kinnamomum*.
Made from the powdered bark of a forest tree species that is native to Sri Lanka but was introduced to Europe by the Dutch, cinnamon is used mostly for sweet dishes in European cuisine, although it is combined with other spices in the savory dishes of Arab and Asian cuisines.

Cloves (*Syzygium aromaticum*)
The Indonesian name for cloves, *cengkeh*, is thought to be derived from the Chinese for "scented nails", alluding to their shape.
Cloves are native to the Moluccas (so-called "spice islands") of South East Asia, and were the first spice to be traded. Each clove is a dried, unopened, flower bud that is pink when fresh and dries to a dark red-brown. Originally used to sweeten the breath, and to flavor and preserve food, cloves are used now, in moderation, to impart their strong flavor to biscuits, cakes and other sweet baking and also added to spice blends and some meat dishes.

Saffron (*Crocus sativus*)
From the Greek *krokos*, meaning a thread.
The bitter spice saffron is made from the dried, bright orange stigmas (female organs) of a species of crocus native to Asia Minor. Known to the Phoenicians, Greeks and Romans, saffron has been cultivated, harvested and greatly valued since ancient times for its medicinal properties and more recently for its culinary use. Its strong taste means that only tiny quantities are required to impart its flavor and fabulous color to food, typically to fish and rice dishes such as *bouillabaisse*, risotto and paella. Genuine saffron swells immediately on landing on water or white wine, and gives its color easily to the liquid.

Juniper (*Juniperus communis*)
This busy evergreen tree is cultivated for its berry-like cones, which gives a distinctive flavor as well as possessing medicinal properties. The main use of juniper berries is to flavor gin. As well as flavoring gin, juniper berries are used in other spirits and beers. Add crushed berries to marinades for game and stuffings for poultry. Various juniper species are used medicinally, although some are too strong for internal use. Juniper has long been credited with cleansing properties. It can remove acid waste from the system and was once believed to cure many illnesses of the digestive system. A powerful external cleanser, juniper can help with eczema, psoriasis, and even cellulite.

Star *anise* (*Illicium verum*)
From the Latin *illicio*, meaning to attract.
Star *anise* is a star-shaped fruit of a small, evergreen tree species from China. The spice has a bitter flavor, which, as the name suggests, is somewhat similar to *anise*. It plays an important role in Chinese cuisine, particularly in meat dishes, used either on its own or as a component of the famous spice mix known as "Five Spice".

Sweet paprika (*Capsicum annuum*)
From the Greek *kapto*, meaning to bite.
In addition to chillies, red and bell peppers, capsicum peppers (which originated in South America) are the source of the bright red powder, paprika, which is now closely associated with the cuisine of Hungary. Made from a variety of capsicum similar to chillies in shape, though not in pungency, paprika comprises powdered flesh (excluding the seeds) and is a key ingredient in goulash, and other Hungarian meat dishes.

Flowers

Pot marigold (*Calendula officinalis*)

From the Latin *kalendae*, meaning "first day of the month".

An attractive, well-known perennial species with single or double flowers, pot marigold is Mediterranean to Near Eastern in origin. With a long history of cultivation, pot marigold was used medicinally by the Egyptians, Greeks, Arabs and Indians who also considered the flowers edible. The petals (the rest of the flower is very bitter and should not be eaten) can be used as a garnish, added to salads and, at the last moment, to cheese dishes. Ground petals produce a paste that adds flavor and color to butter and rice dishes. Pot marigolds can be grown from seed in trays and planted out in spring, in sunny positions with well-drained soil. The flowers should be harvested just as they open, and the petals eaten fresh.

Borage (*Borago officinialis*)

From the Latin *burra*, meaning hairy garment.

An annual herb, native to the Mediterranean, central Europe, the Middle East and North Africa, but now also found in North America, borage is a robust, upright, rather prickly herb with blue or purplish-pink flowers that appear in early summer. The edible flowers can be candied, used as a garnish, or added to salads and cold soups. The flowers are perhaps most well known as an addition with chopped fruits to the English summer drink "Pimms". Borage can be grown from seed in well-drained, preferably light, sandy soil, in sunny positions. The flowers should be harvested when they are just open, and the black central parts of the flowers (stamen and ovary) should be removed before eating.

Nasturtiums (*Tropaeolum majus*)

It is important not to confuse this species with watercress whose Latin name, rather confusingly, is *Nasturtium officinale*.

Tropaeolum derives from the Greek *tropaion*, meaning trophy.

Nasturtium (*Tropaeolum majus*) is an annual plant, native to Peru, whose bright orange-yellow flowers have a characteristic peppery, cress-like taste that makes them interesting and attractive additions to salads, when added in moderation. Nasturtiums can be easily cultivated from seed and thrive in sunny conditions. The flowers should be harvested when they first open, and only used when fresh.

Lavender (*Lavandula angustifolia*)

From the Latin *lavo*, meaning to wash, alluding to its history of use in soap and scents.

A robust, woody herb, native to the mountains of the Mediterranean, lavender is best known as an attractive, sweet-smelling ornamental plant with medicinal and cosmetic uses. However, it also has a culinary role and fresh lavender flowers (harvested at the start of blooming) can be added, in moderation, to jams, ice creams, biscuits and vinegar, and are sometimes crystallized as a garnish. Herbalists use lavender flowers medicinally to treat tension, stress and other nervous disorders. Lavender is easily cultivated from seed or cuttings planted in warm, sunny positions.

Mascarpone

Strictly speaking, this Italian specialty is not really a cheese at all as no starter or rennet is used in its production. Instead the cream is mixed with lemon juice or citric acid and hung in cheesecloth to drain. It used to be freshly made in-store and sold directly from the cheesecloth. Today it is made in factories and packed into sealed cartons.

Mozzarella

Real Mozzarella is made from buffalos' milk in the Campania region of southern Italy. However, there is also a good deal of mozzarella being made from cows' milk in Italy and in a number of other countries such as the USA.

Buffalo-milk mozzarella has a much softer, creamier texture than the more rubbery "cows'-milk" version. It also has a far better taste. Serve it on its own with fresh summer fruit or slice into a salad of tomato or avocado. In cooking, it melts to a lightly stringy texture that is characteristic of good pizza.

Parmigiano-Reggiano

Commonly known as Parmesan, this very hard cheese is made only in certain designated regions of Emilia Romagno in northern Italy. It gets its texture from the long maturation period that may go on for 2 or 3 years. Parmesan is a difficult cheese to cut with a knife so instead it is split open with a special wide-bladed tool and irregular pieces are broken off.

The cheese is thought to be at its peak when you can see tiny tears of moisture glinting on the freshly broken surface. The flavor is wonderfully full and fruity with a salty tang. Serve shaved over well-flavored salad leaves or in small chunks with a dash of traditional balsamic vinegar.

Parmesan should be grated for cooking but avoid buying pre-grated cheese. At best this has lost a good deal of its flavor and at worst it lacks freshness.

Pecorino

This is the general term given to Italian ewes'-milk cheeses. They are compact cheeses which harden with maturity. Each region has its own type. Aromas and flavors change as the cheeses mature, but almost all pecorino has a characteristic touch of lemons and nuts.

Pecorino Romano and Pecorino Sardo are both very salty. They are usually sold when they are very mature and hard. Pecorino Toscano, on the other hand, is often eaten when it is young and fresh with a creamy texture and mild, lemony flavor. The Tuscans serve the fresh cheeses with fava beans in early summer.

Ricotta

This is not really cheese, for it is made from the whey that is left over after the curds have formed in regular cheese making. This Italian specialty is very white in color with a light granular texture. The flavor is mild and sweet.

Ricotta is extremely versatile for it may be served as the cheese course, used in sandwiches and salads or incorporated into cooked dishes. Mixed with salt and pepper or fresh herbs it melts into pasta sauces and it makes an excellent dessert with fresh summer berries.

Roquefort

To be called Roquefort, this great blue cheese must be matured in the caves at Combalou in southern France. It is made from sheep's milk. The cheeses are wrapped in foil and the best are labelled *Surchoix*.

The paste is very white with even, bluish-green veining throughout. The texture is firm and smooth, and almost spreadable. The complex flavor is salty with a tangy finish and undertones of nuts, raisins and fruit.

Serve on its own, as the French do, with a sweet dessert wine such as Sauternes or Barsac. The flavor intensifies with cooking so use sparingly in soups, salads, sauces and other dishes.

Smoked Scamorza

Scamorza is a denser type of mozzarella made in Piedmont as well as in southern Italy. An excellent American example is made by "The Mozzarella Company" in Texas, and it is smoked over pecan shells.

Olive oil

The very best olive oils are unique among cooking oils because they are made directly from the fresh juice of the olive. The fruit is picked, milled and pressed and the resulting juice is separated into oil and water. If this oil is of the required standard it is bottled with no extra processing. This is virgin olive oil.

Olive oils which fail the tests for virgin status are sent to the refinery to be cleaned up to make ordinary olive oil which is flavored with a little virgin oil. This is the oil to use for frying, basting and general cooking.

In fact, there are two grades of virgin olive oil. Extra-virgin oil, which must have an acidity level of less than 1% and virgin oil which must have an acidity level of less than 2%. Both must have a perfect aroma and flavor. These oils are flavoring ingredients in their own right, offering a wealth of different tastes for use in dressings, sauces and marinades as well as in a whole range of other more substantial dishes.

Olive oil has always been prized for its flavor but in recent years it has also come to be valued for its healthy attributes. It is made up largely of monounsaturated fatty acids which are thought to be beneficial in the fight against heart disease and in controlling a variety of other potentially harmful conditions.

Omega 6 essential fatty acids, vitamin E and polyphenol antioxidants add to the benefits of virgin olive oil. The calorie count is fairly high at 120–125 kilocalories per tablespoon, but this is no higher than other fats. So-called light or "lite" olive oil refers to oil that is light in flavor not in calories!

Appreciating olive oil
The requirement for perfect aroma and taste in virgin olive oil does not mean that all olive oils taste the same. Quite the opposite. Olive oil is produced in all the countries of the Mediterranean basin as well as in California, South America, South Africa, Australia and New Zealand, so the scope for choice is enormous.

Styles vary from mild and delicate to bitter and pungent with many graduations in between. Some oils are extremely peppery and others have very little piquancy at all. The choice is purely a matter of personal preference. So, if you can, taste before you buy.

Of course, each style does have its own culinary uses. A very mild and gentle oil will be overwhelmed by the strong flavors of watercress, chicken livers or artichokes. Such an oil would be better served with delicate salad leaves, white fish or breast of chicken.

It is difficult to generalize about the taste and flavor of olive oils from the different growing regions for there will always be an oil which is different. However, French oils tend to be very mild and sweet with fruit flavors and aromas varying from apples and pears to lemons and tomatoes. They are not usually very peppery.

Italy, on the other hand, produces every type of oil imaginable from the light nutty oils of northern Liguria, through the pungent, peppery oils of central Italy to the herbaceous, tomato-flavored oil of Sicily.

Californian oils also vary in style from the lemony mild oils, made from old established table olive varieties, to more herbaceous styles made form newer Italian and Greek olives.

Choosing olive oil
The best olive oil is the freshest and youngest, so look for oils which date from the most recent harvest. Ignore the color of the oil as this is not a good indicator of what you will find in the bottle. Green oils, for example, are not always very pungent and golden yellow oils may not be pepper-free.

Cloudy oil simply means that the oil has not been filtered. The choice between filtered and unfiltered oils is a matter of personal preference. Avoid oils which have been kept in the shop window or on shelves which attract direct sunlight. Olive oil should be stored in a cool dark place, though it is not necessary to refrigerate it.

Some labels carry phrases such as "first pressed", "cold pressed" or "traditional production". These phrases are meaningless. Modern equipment is such that there is no second pressing except at the refinery and no hot pressing. Nor is there any particular virtue in the traditional, hydraulic method of production. If used correctly, each method can produce a first-class extra-virgin oil. The only important words are "extra virgin" and "virgin".

Olive oil is the traditional cooking medium of the Mediterranean and is used as butter and vegetable oils are used in more northerly countries. Do not use virgin olive oil just for dressing salads. Think about using it to finish soups, vegetables, mashed potatoes or grilled fish. Experiment with pot-roasts, baked breads, cookies and cakes or serve in the Mediterranean manner at the beginning of a meal as a dip for bread and raw vegetables.

Mixing and matching virgin olive oil with other ingredients is exciting. Try mixing a strongly herbaceous oil from central Italy with a dash of balsamic vinegar and serve as a dip or salad dressing, use a sweeter French oil to highlight grilled fish fillets with fresh herbs or make a wonderfully moist and flavorsome carrot cake with Californian oil. Experiment with the recipes in this book and then try out your own ideas.

Judy Ridgeway

Wine

The style of any particular wine is determined by the grape variety (or varieties) from which it is produced, the soil and climate in which the grapes are grown and the technique of the winemaker.

Wines are normally sold either by their geographical origin – Bordeaux, Chablis, Soave, Rioja, as is usually the case in the traditional wine-producing areas of Europe or as varietals (by the name of a single or pair of grape varieties), particularly the case for wines from California and the Southern Hemisphere, which may also carry a geographical designation, such as Napa or Coonawarra.

The juice of most grapes is white, so white wine can be produced from either red or white grapes (Champagne is the most common example of a white wine made predominantly from red grapes). Red wines can only be produced from black grapes; the skins, which contain the coloring pigments, are macerated in the fermenting juice for anything up to 2 weeks, to produce color in the wine. The skins also impart tannin to red wines, a natural acid that diminishes in time, but which can make young red wine often taste dry and astringent. However many inexpensive wines are now made by a method of carbonic maceration, much in the traditional style of Beaujolais, which makes them ready to drink within months, if not weeks, of the harvest. *Rosé* wines are produced from a short period of skin contact, 12–48 hours, just long enough to give a subtle color, without the aggressive tannins. Hence *rosé* wines, like most whites, are produced to be drunk while still young and fresh.

The major white grape varieties

Chardonnay is the grape, which produces all great white Burgundy from Chablis to Montrachet, as well as being an important component of Champagne (a Champagne labeled as Blanc de Blancs will have been made exclusively from Chardonnay, as opposed to more commonly being blended with Pinot Noir and/or Pinot Meunier grapes). Chardonnay is widely planted throughout the wine-growing world and both California and Australia produce excellent examples. When the wine is made from low yields it has a rich, buttery character; it is one of the few white varieties that can support fermentation and ageing in oak casks, which gives added complexity to the best wines.

Sauvignon Blanc's home is in Sancerre and Pouilly in the upper Loire valley of France (Pouilly-Fumé is not to be confused with Pouilly-Fuisse, which comes from southern Burgundy and is made from Chardonnay). When grown in cool climates, like the Loire and New Zealand, the wines have a pungent aroma of gooseberries; in hotter climates, such as Australia and California, the wines are less assertive and often herbaceous in character.

Riesling (note the spelling!) produces the best wines in Germany and is also grown in Alsace, Austria, California and Australia, amongst others. The wines are sometimes labeled Rhine or Johannisberg Riesling to distinguish them from Welschriesling, a much inferior grape. Riesling can produce steely dry wines, as in Alsace, right through to late-harvested honeyed, sweet wines from Germany and California.

Semillon is the grape that is principally responsible for the great sweet wines of Sauternes and Barsac in the Bordeaux region of France. Its thin skin makes it susceptible to *Botrytis cinerea* – a form of mold that causes evaporation of much of the water in the grape, thereby increasing the concentration of sugar. It can also produce full-bodied, dry wines with a waxy character, usually the style found in Australian or Californian Semillon.

Muscat is grown throughout the world and can be dry, as is normally the case in Alsace, but is more often found as a sweet wine, with a perfumed, grapey aroma. It is sometimes fortified, often the case in the South of France, Portugal and Australia, and is also responsible for Asti Spumante, the sparkling wine from Piedmont in Italy.

The major red grape varieties

Cabernet-Sauvignon, the standard-bearer for the great wines of Bordeaux, is in fact always blended with other varieties there. But it is grown very successfully, and is often unblended, in most of the major vineyard regions of the world – California, Australia, South America, Italy and Bulgaria. Cabernet-Sauvignons generally have good color and a distinctive blackcurrant fruit flavor.

Merlot is the most widely planted variety in Bordeaux, where it produces the great Pomerols like Petrus and Le Pin. It is also grown successfully elsewhere, particularly in California. Merlots are generally softer and more rounded than Cabernets, with rich, plumy fruit flavors.

Pinot Noir is the cornerstone of red Burgundy and constitutes an important part of the Champagne vineyards. It has not been so successfully planted elsewhere as other classic varieties; it is best suited to cool climates where it generally produces lightly colored wines with soft, flowery, fruit flavors.

Gamay produces the fruity, raspberry-jam tasting wines of Beaujolais, most of which are best drunk within 2–3 years of the vintage. It is also grown in California, not to be confused with Gamay Beaujolais, which is actually a clone of Pinot Noir.

Syrah (or Shiraz) is the grape that produces Hermitage and Côte-Rôtie in the Rhone valley of France, and is extremely successful in Australia; Grange Hermitage generally fetches the highest price of any Australian wine. The wines are deeply colored with a spicy, minerally character.

Nebbiolo is the grape of Piemonte in northwestern Italy where it produces the wines of Barolo and Barbaresco – powerful, high in tannin with flavors of tar and licorice.

Zinfandel, grown almost exclusively in California, produces rich wines full of blackberry fruit, although it is also used for white and "blush" (pink) wines.

Grapes grown in warmer climates will achieve a higher degree of ripeness, with increased sugar levels, which will be converted into higher alcohol in the resulting wine; such wines are often described as being fuller bodied. Grapes from cooler climates will conversely have a lower level of sugar and will subsequently contain less alcohol, and have a higher degree of acidity. Cooler climates are better suited to the production of white, rather than red, wine, which requires a balance of acidity to give a fresh, crisp style. In hotter climates the winemaker often increases acidity artificially in the same way that in cooler climates the alcohol level can be increased by the addition of sugar during the fermentation of the grapes.

An Australian Cabernet-Sauvignon will taste different than a claret from Bordeaux, and a Californian Chardonnay will be different than a white Burgundy, despite being produced from the same grape variety. The reasons are not solely the result of climate and soil but also of winemaking tradition. Practically all the red wines from Bordeaux are a blend of different varieties; over many years it has been found that a blend is superior to a single varietal wine in that particular area. Winemaking practices also vary from country to country, although there are now so many consulting/"flying winemakers" that these differences may diminish.

The principal components of wine are sweetness, acidity, alcohol, fruit flavors and tannin and they are derived from the content of the grape. The riper the grape becomes before it is harvested, the greater the degree of sugar, and the lower the acidity. In most wines the sugar is entirely fermented out into alcohol, but it is possible to retain a degree, to give sweetness to a wine. The greatest sweet white wines are made from grapes that have become concentrated on the vine by the action of a mold, *Botrytis cinerea*, which has allowed much of the water to evaporate. The level of sugar in the grape will also determine the amount of alcohol in the resulting wine; it is, however, quite common for wine producers in cooler climates to add sugar at fermentation to increase the alcoholic degree, a process known as *chaptalization*.

The level of acidity is also influenced by the ripeness of the grape; the less ripe, the greater degree of acidity. Grapes grown in cooler climates will therefore tend to produce wines with higher levels of natural acidity – England, Germany and northern France produce almost exclusively white wine, where the acidity gives the bite and freshness.

The fruit flavors and tannins in wine are derived from the grape variety/varieties used and the soil and climate in which they are grown. Some varieties, such as Muscat, are much more aromatic than others; while some, like the Cabernet-Sauvignon, have thick skins which can give more tannin to a wine. Some wines will be matured in cask for several years; the use of new oak barrels gives a distinctive vanilla character to a wine.

Tasting wine

Wine, when it is poured should look clear and bright in the glass. Some young white wines may have small bubbles of carbon dioxide gas that will enhance the freshness. Light white wines, such as those from Germany, tend to be pale in color while fuller-bodied, richer whites, like Australian Chardonnay, will be a deeper yellow. Most sweet white wines will have a deep golden color. Red wines generally start life with a purple red and take on brick and tawny hues as they age. As with whites, those from warmer climates will tend to have deeper color.

Once poured, and before tasting, one should smell a wine. First, any faults will be apparent to the nose; secondly the bouquet will give a good indication of the taste to come. It helps to swirl the wine around the glass to release the aromas. When tasting, try to move the wine around the mouth and draw in a little air, before swallowing. This gives the wine a chance to reveal its flavors; and the longer they linger in the mouth, the better the quality of the wine.

Storing and serving wine

The ideal storage conditions for wine are an even temperature, around 40°F/12°C, well away from vibration, light, smell and with a relative humidity around 75–80%. Bottles need to be kept on their sides to avoid corks drying out, which would allow air into the bottle and subsequently lead to oxidation.

The best glasses for tasting, and therefore drinking wine, are made of clear, thin glass, narrower at the lip than in the bowl to concentrate the bouquet, and with a stem long enough to keep the hand off the bowl. Glasses, especially for red wine should be generous in size and should not be filled more than two-thirds full to allow

the bouquet to develop as the wine is swirled around the glass.

White and *rosé* wines should be served around 24°F/7°C; any colder and the bouquet and flavor will be lost. Sparkling wines can, however, be served a little cooler, which helps to reduce the pressure of the gas in the bottle. Most red wines are best served around 48°F/14°C but some lighter styles, like Beaujolais and Valpolicella are best served cool (34–40°F/10–12°C) and very full-bodied wines, like Barolo or Australian Shiraz can be served up to 55°F/16°C. Most red wines, apart from the lighter styles, benefit from being opened up to 2 hours before serving.

Red wines, which have spent many years maturing, will generally need decanting to separate them from the sediment that has settled in the bottle. White wines, which might show a crystalline deposit, do not need decanting; it is only a natural deposit of tartaric acid crystals that settle comfortably in the bottle or glass. Fortunately, very few wines today are faulty; the most common are those which are corked, the result of a tainted cork which renders the wine woody and musty, and those which have become oxidized, a problem mostly affecting white wines which have been badly stored, or kept too long. Once a bottle has been opened it should not kept for more than a day or two; the wine will deteriorate quite quickly.

Wine and food matching

Many food and wine combinations are just the result of history and/or geography; not many would naturally choose to drink Sauternes, a rich, sweet white wine, with *foie gras*, but it remains one of the classic combinations. The two basic criteria to follow are complement and contrast. A strong or spicy tasting food will overpower a light wine in the same way that a rich, full-bodied wine will overwhelm light foods; Chablis is perfect with shellfish, but would not stand up to game. Good contrasts would be a wine made from Sauvignon Blanc, with high acidity, and smoked salmon, which is naturally oily, or red Bordeaux, with its dry tannins, and lamb, which is sweet and fatty. Garlic kills the aroma and taste of red wine so a dish of escargot should always be accompanied by white wine.

When choosing wines to match specific dishes, remember it is not just a question of selecting a wine to go with a particular meat or fish; the sauce in which they are cooked can be even more important. Cream- or butter-based sauces usually need wines with good acidity rather than high alcohol to cut the richness. Some tastes are almost impossible to match, such as vinegar, the natural antithesis of wine. The best answer is probably a full-bodied, dry white with low acidity. Chocolate can also distort the flavor of most wines, but a sweet, fortified Muscat, such as those from Australia or California, will be a fine accompaniment. Most wines will taste very different when drunk with food than when tasted on their own. After champagne be sure to cleanse your palate with a bit of bread and a mouthful of water before testing a red wine.

The increasing consumption of wine on its own has contributed to the popularity of New World wines, many of which, with their ripe, sweet fruit flavors, are at their best with simple roast or grilled dishes. By contrast, many Italian red wines can taste somewhat dry and astringent on their own, but soften dramatically when drunk with a cuisine based on olive oil.

If you are serving several different wines during the course of a meal, there are really three criteria to try and follow: dry before sweet, light before fuller bodied and young before old.

Richard Harvey

269

London's Specialty Food Stores

Butchers

A. S. Portwine & Son
24 Earlham Street
London WC2H 9LN
Tel: 020 7836 2353
Fax: 020 7813 0313
British butcher, organic

Butcher & Edmonds
1–3 Grand Avenue
Leadenhall Market
London EC3V 1LR
Tel: 020 7626 5816/
020 7623 5946
Butcher and game dealer

C. Lidgate
110 Holland Park Avenue
London W11 4UA
Tel: 020 7727 8243
Fax: 020 7229 7160
Butcher, game dealer and organic

Frank Godfrey
7 Highbury Park
London N5 1QT
Tel/Fax: 020 7226 9904
Butcher, free range and organic

Freeman's Butchers
9 Topsfield Parade
London N8 8PR
Tel: 020 8340 3100
Butcher, game dealer and organic

Kingsland Edwardian Butcher
140 Portobello Road
London W11 2DZ
Tel: 020 7727 6067
Fax: 020 7727 0706
Butcher, game dealer and organic

Randalls
113 Wandsworth Bridge Road
London SW6 2TE
Tel: 020 7736 3426
Butcher

French

Bagatelle Boutique
44 Harrington Road
London SW7 3NB
Tel: 020 7584 2432
Fax: 020 7591 0517
French bakery, pâtisserie and delicatessen

Villandry
170 Great Portland Street
London W1N 5TB
Tel: 020 7631 3131
Fax: 020 7631 3030
Specialist French food hall

French and Italian

Rosslyn Delicatessen
56 Rosslyn Hill
London NW3 1ND
Tel: 020 7794 9210
Fax: 020 7794 6828
French and Italian delicatessen

Italian

Belsize Village Delicatessen
39 Belsize Lane
London NW3 5AS
Tel: 020 7794 4258

Carluccio's
28a Neal Street
London WC2 9PS
Tel: 020 7240 1487
Fax: 020 74971361
Italian delicatessen

Enzo Tartarelli
1 Sidmouth Parade
Sidmouth Road
London NW2 5HG
Tel: 020 8459 1952
Italian butcher, delicatessen and greengrocer

Fratelli Camisa
53 Charlotte Street
London W1P 1LA
Tel: 020 7255 1240
Italian delicatessen

G. Gazzano & Sons
167–169 Farringdon Road
London EC1R 3AL
Tel: 020 7837 1586
Italian delicatessen

I. Camisa
61 Old Compton Street
London W1V 5PN
Tel: 020 7437 76410
Italian delicatessen

Lina Stores
18 Brewer Street
London W1R 3FS
Tel: 020 7437 6482
Italian delicatessen

Luigi's
349 Fulham Road
London SW3 3DZ
Tel: 020 7352 7739
Italian delicatessen

Specialty Cheese Shops

Barstow & Barr
32/34 Earl's Court Road
London W8 6EJ
Tel/Fax: 020 7937 8004

La Fromagerie
30 Highbury Park
London N5 2AA
Tel/Fax: 020 7359 7440

Neal's Yard Dairy
17 Short's Gardens
London WC2H 9AT
Tel: 020 7379 7646
Fax: 020 7240 2442

Paxton & Whitfield
93 Jermyn Street
London SW1Y 6JE
Tel: 020 7930 0259
Fax: 020 7321 0621

Bluebird Store Ltd
350 King's Road
London SW3 5UU
Tel: 020 7559 1000
Fax: 020 7559 1111
www.conran.co.uk
Gourmet food hall

'Borough Food Market'
Borough Market
London SE1 9AB
For more information phone
Neal's Yard Dairy on Tel: 020
7645 3550
*Dedicated food market held every
Friday and Saturday. Various
growers, farmers, wholesalers and
food producers come from around
the country to sell their wares.*

Felicitous
19 Kensington Park Road
London W11 2EU
Tel: 020 7243 4050
Fax: 020 7243 4052
*Delicatessen with a fascinating
variety of fresh and dried pasta*

Harrods
Brompton Road
London SW1X 7XL
Tel: 020 7730 1234
Fax: 020 7893 8945/581 0470
Gourmet food hall

Harvey Nichols & Co Ltd
Fifth Floor – The Food Market
109–125 Knightsbridge
London SW1X 7RJ
Tel: 020 7235 5000
Fax: 020 7235 5020
Gourmet food hall

Partridges of Sloane Street
www.partridges.co.uk
132–134 Sloane Street
London SW1X 9AT
Tel: 020 7730 0651
Fax: 020 7730 7104

Partridges of Kensington
17–23 Gloucester Road
London SW7 4PC
Tel: 020 7581 0535
Fax: 020 7581 3449

The Rosslyn Delicatessen
www.diliorsslyn.co.uk
56 Rosslyn Hill
Hampstead
London NW3 1ND
Tel: 020 7794 9210
Fax: 020 7794 6828

Fortnum and Mason
181 Piccadilly Road
London W1
Tel: 020 7734 8040

Selfridges
Oxford Street
London W1
Tel: 020 7629 1234

Index of French recipes

Index of Italian recipes

Judy Ridgeway

Judy Ridgeway is an author, journalist and broadcaster specializing in all aspects of taste and flavor, with particular emphasis on olive oil, cheese and wine.

Her fifty-plus books include *The Olive Oil Companion*, *The Connoisseur's Cheese Guide* and *The Cheese Companion*, all of which have been published in both the US and the UK.

Taste and flavor are also keynotes of publications such as *The Wine Tasting Class* which was nominated for the 1977 Julia Child Awards in America, her paper on "Taste and Flavor in Olive Oil" commissioned by the European Union and her latest book with Patrick Hanford – *The Optimum Nutrition Cookbook*.

She also writes regularly for a wide variety of women's and general interest magazines and appears on national and local television and radio. She conducts cheese, wine and olive-oil tasting for consumer groups and judges olive oil at international level.

She is a member of the Circle of Wine Writers and the Guild of Food Writers. She is also a Companion of the French Guilde des Fromagers, Confrérie de Saint-Uguzon.

Richard Harvey

Richard spent several of his early childhood years in Italy, which doubtless sowed the seeds for his subsequent love of food and wine.

Trained as an architect, he left after a year and spent a few months working for Oddbins (British chain of specialty wine stores), before joining Prue Leith's catering business in 1972. As his passion for wine developed, he decided to join the wine trade in 1974 and the following year went to run the Grant of St James's School of Wine for two years. In 1978, he set up his own business, Richard Harvey Wines, and in 1982 became a Master of Wine. From 1988 to 1995 Richard ran wine courses at Leith's School of Food and Wine and wrote *Leith's Guide to Wine*, published by Bloomsbury in 1995. As well as running his own business, specializing in Bordeaux, he is a consultant to Bonham's auctioneers for their wine sales.

Sasha Barrow, PhD

Originally trained as a botanist, Sasha Barrow currently works as an economic botanist focusing on the wide range of uses of plants by different people around the world. Through her work she has traveled widely in Asia where she has also worked in the fields of biodiversity, conservation and sustainable development. Back at home in the UK, she has worked in developing and producing various environmental publications.

Thierry Cardineau

Thierry is native to France and started his photographic career in the late eighties. He is a leading ski photographer, traveling worldwide for the past ten years in most places where snow can be found.

Now established in both France and the United Kingdom, he is renowned for his interior photography of luxury villas and chalets. Food photography is the latest addition to Thierry's portfolio.

Clarissa Hyman

Clarissa Hyman was born into a family of deli owners and very good eaters in Manchester, England. Whilst reading psychology at university, she spent a summer in Rome where she began a life-long passion for Italian food, shoes and men, whoops, culture. She worked as a producer and researcher for Granada TV before embarking on a second career as a food and travel writer. She has won or been shortlisted for several major awards, and in 2000 was honored as "Food Journalist of the Year" by the Guild of Food Writers in their Annual Awards. Her first book, *Cucina Siciliana* will be published by ConranOctopus in 2002. She still lives in Manchester, but dreams of the Mediterranean.

Here's how to contact us:

Luxury Destinations Ltd
The Courtyard Suite
Hambledon House
Vann Lane
Hambledon
Surrey GU8 4HW
United Kingdom

Toll-free from U.S.:
1.888.254.1070
International direct dial:
+44.1428.68.51.40
Fax:
+44.1428.68.34.24

Website:
www.rhodeschoolofcuisine.com
www.luxurypropertyrentals.com
Email: info@rhodeschoolofcuisine.com

How it all got started

Once upon a time in Giverny, Terri asked me "Why not have a cooking school? You have an incredible French chef, brilliant properties, why not?"

Well that made me think of my Dad who'd run a fast *hors d'oeuvres* business during the thirties, with my aunt Irma and James Beard for partners. There is indeed a history of cuisine in the family, I reflected. My father William Rhode, even wrote cookbooks and was editor of *Gourmet* magazine when it was getting started in the forties. So it all started in Monet's gardens of Giverny, or possibly even in New York dateline 1936 – who knows?

So James, William and Irma, the tradition continues wherever you are!

Mike

RHODE SCHOOL of CUISINE

RSC